A Testimony of Life's Journey: Breaking the Silence

All Scripture quotations are taken from the King James Translation Holy Bible.

Published by Minister Judy Linzy

ISBN – 9781092293051

Pictures provided by Pixabay.com and are used for illustrative purposes only.

For information contact:
Judy C. Linzy
(210) 537-8202

Email: judylinzy65@gmail.com

A Testimony of Life's Journey: Breaking the Silence

by

Minister & Creative Image Author

Judy C. Linzy

"Flying the high road of life.

Ordained Ministerial of Religion

Divined, Dignified & Distinguished Minister

Minister Judy Linzy was born in the state of Louisiana, raised in a small-town named New Iberia. Graduated from New Iberia Senior High in 1971, afterwards, she went to McKinney Job Corps in Texas, to further her education. She was employed as a Certified Nursing Assistant for six years, a Provider for the handicap for ten years, worked on the Iberia Parish School Board for four years, and retired after three years as an infant daycare teacher.

Divined, Dignified & Distinguished Minister

Ms. Linzy is a powerful leader with exceptional skills in spiritual divinity. Minister Linzy represents the biblical foundation as the pillar of her church. She expressed her interest in inspirational empowerment and community leadership.

As a young child, she received confidence and strength, to move forward while facing incriminating circumstances. She had a major concern for individuals that struggled from trials, tribulations, and troubles. Her passion is to spiritually educate them and set them free from within. Her desire is to show others a different outlook on life.

Divined, Dignified & Distinguished Minister

Minister Linzy stated, "my aim is to assure them; they would rise above the pain they endured. God has the power to take us from mental anguish, to an elevation of increased purpose. We learn how to transform, and rejuvenate our life."

"Lastly, we are often tested to see if we value, the plan God has prepared for us. Will we pass the test? Are we obedient to his word? Do we accept and complete task that we are assigned to do? Do we talk instead of listening? Once we have accomplished his principles; the heavy burdens that weighed our heart and mind down, would lead us towards success."

Author's Sneak Peak

"A Testimony of Life's Journey: Breaking the Silence," is a short story related to real-life facts. This book is powerful and filled with an abundance of knowledge. You will learn the truth, about the heartfelt dissatisfying situations of innocence children, that were emotionally abused by the sins of the devil.

People need to know if they commit their life to God, and trust him, he'll set them free. He is the only one, that has the power to set us free to fly like an eagle. He gives us childlike faith to where we can look to him for all our help.

Trust in the Lord with all your heart, lean not to your own understanding and in all your ways acknowledge him and he will direct your path. No one, young or old, must live in the clutches of the dark world.

I give all glory, honor and praise to our almighty God for placing in me, even as a child, the ability to share my hurt and pain. I am so thankful; my spirit is free!

<u>EXPRESSION OF GRATITUDE</u>

I reverence all praises to **God** for allowing me the opportunity to share the truth, about the hidden life of turmoil and abuse.

I would like to acknowledge my loving husband, **Edward Linzy** (deceased) for encouraging me to never give up on the blessings God created for me. Secondly, I'm grateful for my father, **Eugene Charles, Sr. (deceased),** for loving me, and enhancing my knowledge, and encouraging me to be a warrior in my life.

I'm grateful for my children, **Willie Morton, Jr.** (son) & **Kizzy Londo** (daughter) for encouraging me to reach for the stars.

My grandchildren, **Deante Morton, Precious Morton, Railyn Morton, Harmony Morton, Serenity Morton, Amari Morton, Jamond Polk, Jr., Jamod Polk, Jamiracle Polk, Stephen Londo** and **Jahiem Londo, Makeia Edwards,** Lastly, my great grandchildren, **Kaiden J. E. Morton**, **Jaiden Robertson**, and **JaLeigha Robertson.**

SPECIAL ACKNOWLEDGEMENTS

Pastor Apostle Hervey Beal, and the beautiful **Elect Lady Prophetess Apostle Linda Beal,** thank you for encouraging me to listen when God speak, and to follow his lead.

Lastly, I would like to thank **Vivian D. Lewis, Creative Image Motivational Writer** for encouraging me, to keep running the race for success...keep pushing forward.

Thanks to all for the big PUSH!

TABLES OF CONTENTS

Sometimes the heart sees, what's invisible to the eye."

"A loving heart is the beginning of all knowledge."

"A kind heart is a foundation of gladness, making everything in its vicinity freshen into smiles."

MOMENTS OF TRUTH

Chap. 1

Everyone is born with direction and filled with the expression of God's grace. I came forth with the sole purpose, of providing spiritual empowerment, to people that fell short along life's way. God created us to represent his principles, and reach out to those that need to feel his unveiling love.

MOMENTS OF TRUTH

My mother told me a nurse prayed for me, on the day of my birth. She also said, God had already shown her, the distinguished qualities I would adapt to, through the milestones of life. I would blossom with integrity, passion, and leadership. I thank God for the divined greatness of that nurse.

James 5:16 says, "The prayer of a righteous person is powerful and effective." My intellectual skills are highly developed, with the ability to minister to people that have been scorned by trials, tribulations, and troubles. Proverbs 3:5-6 reads, **"Trust in the Lord with all thine heart; and lean not unto thine own understanding."** God equipped us with the proper resources, that would allow us to walk the path he designed. As a child, I didn't get to know him, but I gained knowledge, through life's learning. I always felt his presence, and it was refreshing.

MOMENTS OF TRUTH

The home I lived in wasn't great, I didn't have any adult, I could talk to. Due to unknown reasons, I lived with my father and his mate; but that was unethical. I knew he loved me, but he worked all the time. I couldn't trust anyone else, so I talked to God. Even though I didn't know him, I remember the little that my mother taught me. She said, God knows the beginning, and the end of what we need; he is the Alpha and the Omega.

Jeremiah 1:5 states, "I knew you before I formed you in your mother's womb. Before you were born I set you apart, and appointed you as my spokesman to the world."

He even protects his fetus, he gave the mother the ability to nourish, and communicate with her unborn offspring. Then, when the baby is born, bonding will become inevitable.

MOMENTS OF TRUTH

When we come into the world, the first one we see is our parents. We look for them to nurture, and teach us the necessities of life. **(Everything should start from home)** They are responsible to teach us how to be respectful in society. Many parents lack knowledge, and the understanding, of being a model citizen. They must obey laws, and set a good example for their children to follow.

They are also supposed to instill positive beliefs, and not inflict their bad habits upon them. Parents must be grounded in Christ before spiritual principles can be taught to their children. Also, their heart must be embedded with purity and divined manners. It is their duty to introduce, and teach them about our heavenly father. Babies are born without any spiritual knowledge and must be taught the do's and don't, of life. We trust our parents to provide for us.

Five values, parents should teach their children at a young age.

Value #1: Honesty – Parents must be a model of truthfulness, so their children will follow the same pattern.

Value #2: Justice – Insist that children make amends.

Value #3: Determination – Encourage them to never give up, and to challenge their knowledge.

Value #4: Consideration – teach them to not be selfish, and to care about the feelings of others.

Value #5: Love – Teach them to love and not hate.

MOMENTS OF TRUTH

When I was young; I didn't know anything until I researched the truth; I learned the hard way. I found out that we are supposed to live by divined morals, standards, and principles. We must respect our elders and our peers. The truth was inherited by our ancestors; it was their line of duty, to rear children without foolish antics.

Somewhere down the line, we've lost the proper way of rearing our children. We disconnected from our roots and moved into unfamiliar territory. It is said, **"we fall down, but we don't have to stay down, the choice is ours."**

Romans 8:28 "And we know that God causes everything to work together, for the good of those who love him, and are called according to his purpose for them."

MOMENTS OF TRUTH

It's not too late to start doing what's right, once we learn the truth, move forward to help others. As soon as my eyes were opened to the truth, I began teaching my children, the spiritual and natural aspects of life. For example, I let them know, they could always confide in me. I also asked them very important questions, some were more disturbing than others. I wanted them to be educated about the treacherous behaviors of the devil.

I made them understand the wonderful pleasures, that come from the grace of God. I wanted them to understand, with Him, they would be free in their mind. I also showed them the opposing side of not allowing him to work generously within; I told them, they would be trapped and imprisoned. The generations have failed to give children the utmost spiritual nourishment. Some parents are not teaching religion in the home.

MOMENTS OF TRUTH

We as parents, are not providing great skills when we tell them, to do as I say, and then, they watch us do negative things. That is an unteachable behavior, which is ruthless. Adults, should be respectful, and show their children proper structure. Evil spirits, does not belong in the lives of God's children. We must have a spiritual connection, in order to follow the path of righteousness. Adhering to the principles of God's word, is greatness.

It's our job to teach our children, life skills. We must assure them, that's where our inner stability comes from. Many times, we tell our children to do things, they may not understand, and they become confused. Like I said before, it is our duty, as parents, to use the proper wording, and explain as many times needed, until the child understands. I have known parents to get angry and grab a belt, and start pouncing on them.

MOMENTS OF TRUTH

Abuse is never right, and against our heavenly father's principles. Hitting a child with aggression is forbidden. Physical abuse is defined as, "any non-accidental physical injury to an individual. Striking, kicking, burning, or biting, or any other action, is a physical form. Abuse could result in a physical impairment of the child. Neglect is defined as the failure of a parent, or any person with the responsibility, to provide basic necessities.

Child abuse, is termed as any type of cruelty inflicted, physically, emotionally and sexually, to name a few. Severe punishment exist for offenders that commit such a cruel act. If an adult fail to provide a proper living foundation, they will be executed to the full extent of the law. Abuse is never right and if our behavior is not good, we can't expect our children to be right. Our childhood hurts, could stifle the growth of our children.

MOMENTS OF TRUTH

I was punched in my face as a child, by an adult; blood came streaming down, and I incurred a big gash on the side of my eye. I was knocked to the floor, and I could hardly see. I got up slowly, looked around, and wondered what I did wrong. I didn't understand, so I blamed myself. Parents we should never attack our children, it is unethical and immoral. There is no justification for that type behavior. A loving parent will admit their faults and apologize to the child for his/her disobedience.

We must have an open communication with our children at all times. We must be sincere, caring, and loyal, when providing structure; anger is never the solution. Some parents lack skills, so how can they teach their children?

Hosea 4:6 states, "My people are being destroyed because they don't know me."

MOMENTS OF TRUTH

I couldn't understand why I wasn’t raised by both of my parents, I felt all alone; I had no one to confide in. There were other adults that occupied our home, but they were no good. There were so many restrictions, we were not allowed, to be in an adult’s presence, unless it was time to eat. We had a specific place to play, and the older siblings took care of the younger ones, while the adults gathered in another area of the yard; they showed no interest in us.

I loved my father but he wasn't home most of the time; all he did was work. The other adults showed no concern; they sent us to school and didn't care what happened. I tried my best to understand, why they lived in our home and didn't love us; I couldn't see the reason. They caused nothing but stress and fear; they were scary people. I was glad to go to school because my teacher cared, and I felt safe.

MOMENTS OF TRUTH

Parents, it is our responsibility to take care of our children. We should never allow any other adults, to be in our home that has hatred within them. They should never have to go to school, and look for the teachers to be their parent figure. Their job is to provide education, and developmental skills **(knowledge is power)**. A nurturing parent will follow behind the educator and teach fundamentals of being productive in society.

We must take all the time needed to raise our children, so they will learn how to act in certain environments **(discipline is essential)**. As a child, I didn't have the opportunity to learn through love; I encountered an tremendous amount of abuse. I remember at age five, I told myself, I wanted to be the perfect child, no lying, stealing and/or showing disrespect. That didn't work though, I was treated like a slave.

MOMENTS OF TRUTH

I was treated very cruel, by one particular adult, that lived in our home. I didn’t understand what the problem was, and why I was always being accused, of things I didn't do. Other children lived in the home, but I was the one always in trouble. I was torn apart in my mind because I didn't know how to get to the root of it. I wanted to tell my father, but I didn't want to cause any more problems. If I had mentioned it to the other adults, I would have been ignored.

I got angry and my attitude changed, I became rebellious. I said, “since I'm being accused, I might as well, do wrong.” Right then, I opened the door and invited sin into my life. I didn't know I was getting into deeper trouble, I just wanted revenge. I experienced extreme physical and mental weakness; I wasn't happy at all. I regret the things I done, I should have never, allowed the enemy to get the best of me.

MOMENTS OF TRUTH

When I told God I wanted to be the perfect child, I was sincere, but the devil took control. I listened to the wrong spirit, and let my anger get the best of me. That negative experience taught me, that everything I do, is a choice, whether its good or bad. Unwise decisions could destroy more than my life; my children will suffer as well. Adults, I must share my words of wisdom:

"When we provoke our children, God is not pleased. They came into the world to be nurtured by us, if we do not fulfill our duties, we will be punished. It is wrong to mistreat an innocence child; they do not deserve inhumane cruelty. When a parent or an adult figure is disobedient, God frowns, and consequences are immediately given; watch what you do."

MOMENTS OF TRUTH

At first, I didn't think grown-ups made mistakes, even though I saw many. After I started growing up and learning a different way, I had to wash my mind, with the word of God. I needed a daily renewal, so I could be refreshed with righteous thoughts. I thank God for strengthening my spirit, and teaching me how to meditate on his word. Some women lack understanding, and the ability to show love towards their offspring.

There is a curse that was passed down from one generation to another, because of a rebellion against God. If your family line is marked by divorce, incest, poverty, anger, or other ungodly patterns, you're likely to be under a curse. We learned from our parents, they learned from their parents and the curse continued. Negative choices are never good, but changes can be made.

Deuteronomy 30:19 says, "we can either choose life and blessings, or death and cursing."

MOMENTS OF TRUTH

I learned, because of the curse I lived under, prayer was necessary. I didn't know everything, but I knew I could talk to God. I asked him for protection, guidance, strength, and all positive motives. I also asked him to deliver me from the demon that lived in our home.

When I was born, I didn't have any knowledge of living unjustly, but after years, watching the adults, I knew they were cursed too; they were ruthless. There are ***Spiritual Must Be's***, that parents must adhere to; the adults in our home failed all of them.

A. Children must be loved, parents must be trustworthy.

B. Children must be nurtured, parents must be mature, and give their children a firm foundation to stand on.

MOMENTS OF TRUTH

Parent's you are the one that holds the key to your child's positive learning. Open the door and give them a life of happiness, joy, peace, and love **(Fruits of the Spirit)**. No child should be afraid of their parents. They should be able to move freely, without the feeling of being attacked. Parents are supposed to nurture their children and provide an environment, that is comfortable and peaceful.

Children should never be afraid to come to you; corporal punishment should never cross your mind. All of the adults I lived under, was rude, abusive, unethical and illiterate; they had no education. I clearly didn't understand why they lived with my father, brother and I. They kept up a lot of noise, hollering at the kids all the time; the feeling was unreal. I decided, no matter how they treated me, when I learned how to read and write, I would teach them.

I knew they were people, that probably didn't get the opportunity to enhance their educational abilities; maybe that was the reason for their dysfunctional behavior. I remember this like it was yesterday, when I went to second grade, I advanced exceptionally well. I was so excited, I signed up right away to work with the seniors. I helped them write letters, read books, and even taught some of them how to write.

They couldn't believe, at my age, I was so knowledgeable. One day I was assigned to help a small group, every one was nice but one lady. She spoke very aggressively towards me, not realizing I was just a child. her spirit was unclean. For her to be old, she was out of control and her spirit was unclean. Her behavior made me feel like I was at home. I ignored her actions, because I wanted my school project to be great. I asked her if I could help her in any way.

She stared at me for a long while, then answered. In a soft whispering voice, she asked me if I could help her find her father. Despite the way she treated me, I told her I would help her. For the first time, I saw her crack a smile, I was happy from then on. The next day it was easy talking to her; she made me happy. I asked her her name, and she said, “Mundai.” I told her she had a beautiful name, and then I asked her, why she was named after the first day of the week.

She told me, her mother said, she was born on a Monday, the same day of her birthday. I got teary eyed, cause I didn't live with my mother. She then told me, no one would help her find her father, they would always look over her. She then asked me, “what's your name?” I said, “Judy.” She told me my name was pretty, just like me. I thanked her and said, “I'm going to help you.”

She looked at me strange, because she probably thought, since I was a little girl, I had no knowledge. I asked Mundai, where did her father live, she told me, the last time she talked to him, he lived in California. I was determined to make her think differently about young people, so I asked my teacher for guidance. She told me exactly what to do, and I started to work immediately.

All of a sudden, I had a thought, since she was elderly, her father could have been deceased. I decided to start my research anyway, so I could find out the truth. I researched for several months, to ensure I had the right person. I was surprised, when I heard back from him, he said, he tried to find his daughter as well. He listed his phone number, so I called him; he was surprised to know I was a small child. I told him, his daughter really want to see him.

I also asked him, if he was able to travel, he told me, he had an assistant and could go anywhere he wanted to go. I didn't tell her anything, until her father was wheeled into the building. To see the smile on her face, warmed my heart; she was so excited. From that point on, she smiled freely, her heart was soft. She told everyone that I had outstanding skills, as a young girl. After I completed my task, I learned to continue treating people, the way I wanted to be treated; I chose to love instead of hate.

Adults need to understand, love is an action word and must be shown. I was so happy when I saw her smile, her attitude had changed. I enjoyed seeing her happy, and not frowning. Then I had a not so great thought, about the conditions I lived under. The hatred shown by my fathers mate, was outrageous. She frowned every day unless she was doing something devilish.

She had a weird sounding laugh; that was scary. I wanted to ask her if I could help her read, but I wasn't so sure, she wanted me to. She looked at me like she wanted to kill me, but I didn't pay any attention. Even though I didn't understand what the Bible was all about, I knew that lady should have treated me better. All of a sudden, I heard, “talk to her.” I didn't like those words, talk to her for what, I'm the child. She should be nurturing me instead of hurting me.

I wondered if she was angry because she didn't have good parents. Maybe her mother and father treated her bad, and that made her bitter. I heard it again, “talk to her.” I surely didn't want to strike up a conversation, with a frowning sad woman. I then thought, I have to be obedient, so later that evening, I said, “ma'am may I teach you how to read?” She looked at me, and lifted her arm to hit me, but my father walked into the room.

MOMENTS OF TRUTH

Jesus said to me, "No matter what comes your way, continue to be who you are, and astonish this mean old world with your acts of kindness. Never let the burdens of devilish acts, weigh you down. Always trust and believe in me, and I will direct your path towards a safe place of happiness."

I tried my best to obey God's word, but that didn't work. After a while, I had a different feeling within, I learned how to deal with the negativity. I tried again, to offer my help to all the adults, including her. Several of them were grateful, but she declined.

MOMENTS OF TRUTH

People that know “Jesus is Love,” has an array of pleasing character. They cheerfully express their feelings, and don't tear others down. Their character will reflect how they feel inside; they are pleasant to communicate with. As an adult, I learned, being negative, bitter, or trying to get even, is a recipe for disaster. Your tact must remain positive, so you can reap rewards, instead of consequences.

A negative action will cause you pain. In other words, trying to prove a point, will cause hurtful pain, within yourself; revenge is worse. Certainly, there were times, I felt like I should have confronted the bad people, but I was reminded, to hold my tongue. I must remember Christ is my peacemaker; and to never lower my standards. The way to change a negative, is with a positive; that is everlasting.
“Christ is the peacemaker.”

MOMENTS OF TRUTH

When I turned a teenager, I went through many trials, tribulations, and troubles. I was in disbelief about my facial appearance. I thought about having a transformation; I felt I was not pleasing to others. I also thought about wearing a mask, to cover the scars that were inflicted on my body. Many nights I cried and prayed, until I learned how to rise above the hurtful feelings. I was taught by my heavenly father, to not worry about what the flesh portrayed.

He said, everyone had some type of infliction, whether emotional or physical; it started on the inside and gravitated to the outside, or vice versa. When a person truly loves you, the scars are over looked; the heart is what counts.

My question is: Do parents treat the child that is not as appealing, the same as the others? Do parents have a favorite child, if so, why?

MOMENTS OF TRUTH

I know those are hard questions to answer, but to be truthful, some parents do make a difference between their children. In the eyes of God, we are the same, he loves us as one. It took a while for it to sink in, but one day I understood what he was saying. Some people had more scars than I did, I saw physical, mental, and emotional wounds. I learned that humans pay more attention to what they see, but often forget the inside could be on the verge of self destruction.

God favors our heart, a person can have a flawless look, but if their heart is not appealing; they are still considered ugly. He told me to rise above the evil, and soar like an eagle. I understood what I was told, but I just couldn't get past the mean cruel things, that always happened at home. I remember when I tried to get revenge, towards my fathers mate, but I got caught and was punished.

I knew I was wrong, but at the time, it felt right. I wanted to show her how wrong she had been, for treating me worse than the other children. Every time I tried to talk to her, she showed no interest, and that kept me angry.

"Disobedience is wrongly hearing the word. The Bible says to pay attention to the knowledge of truth not of facts."

One evening after school, I came home and told her my shoes had came apart; she immediately spoke negative. She said hateful things, like I purposely tore them up. I couldn't understand why she always made me feel like I was lying. As I was talking to her, I saw the hatred in her eyes. She didn't show any concern, and I had to go to school the next day. My father was out of town, working, so I had no choice but to tell her; She didn't seem to care, because the next morning, my situation was still the same.

She made me go to school, with no shoes, just a pair of socks. She also made me wear pants, which was against school policy. I was embarrassed because the students laughed at me. As soon as I got to school, I had to go to the office; the principal punished me. He didn't even try to listen, to the reason why, I was out of my regular uniform. I saw how he was fixated on being powerful, instead of helpful. Being a little girl, I didn't know how to defend myself, I just took the rough treatment.

Quietly I said, “why did she make me go to school like that, she knew the dress code?” I felt like she didn't believe me, when I told her what happened to my shoes. I told the truth, but that didn't matter to her. I was surprised that my father allowed her to treat me so cruel; he must not have known. I had not seen him, but I knew she probably had heard from him.

MOMENTS OF TRUTH

After everything died down, she decided to have a conversation with my brother and me. She told us how she wanted us to address her. She said, "you can call me step-mother." I thought that was rude, so I sat quietly for a long while, just looking at the floor. I then responded, "I don't know what brother is going to say, but as for me, you're not my mother." She got quiet and had the expression of a pit bull; she was furious.

She should have been ashamed, to ask me that garbage. Even though she left me in the care of my father; I only had one mother. I remember the last words she said, before leaving me with him, it was, "I love you, Judy; I will be back." Those words kept me connected to her, even though I didn't see her for quite a while.

No one could take my mother's place in my heart, I loved her, and only her. She brought me into the world, and I will love her forever. I didn't intentionally try to provoke the lady, I just politely refused. I was honest with her and continued to be respectful, but her attitude showed me, she didn't like me. I guess she thought, I was speaking sarcastic, so she continued to treat me differently from the other children.

I asked God to show me, what the problem was, and it finally appeared. She remained distant and angry, because I didn't give her the response she expected. I didn't like it, because she was an abuser and living in our home; her presence kept me on edge. She was sneaky and conniving, so her cruelty was not seen. She was good at scheming and being secretive. As I said before, my father worked all the time, so I didn't get to see him much.

MOMENTS OF TRUTH

Abuse is a serious matter, it is often covered up, because of being fearful, that the attacker could retaliate. The victim thinks, staying quiet is the best way, but that is far from the truth. There's nothing hidden, that won't be revealed. Everything done in dark, will always come to light, no matter how long it takes.

"But those with an evil heart seem to have talent for destroying beautiful which is about to bloom."

~Cynthia Rylant

"God will curse the wicked!"

Proverbs 3:31-33 – Do not envy the violent people; don't copy their ways. For the Lord detests the perverse, but takes the upright into his confidence. The Lord's curse is on the house of the wicked, but he blesses the home of the righteous.

Which one do I choose?

EVIL SPIRITS

Chap. II

I had a major concern because my father's friend, I didn’t know how to make it better. I wanted her out of our home, because she had a negative spirit. I felt uncomfortable, because I didn't know, if she would commit an evil attack, when I was sleep. I was haunted all the time, and I had nightmares. I also dreamed about a red devil with a long tail, horns, and pitchfork.

It was like a monster haunting; taunting, and touching my skin, all the time. Evil spirits lurk inside of a sinner, they do not care how others are treated. They possess filthy disgusting character, with no remorse. Instead of offering to help the person, they’ll laugh and talk about them. They feel like they're on top, and can't be touched. That statement is far from the truth, God despise prideful arrogant people.

EVIL SPIRITS

He sits high and has respect for the low, he favors those that humble their heart for others. God is happy when acts of kindness, is shown towards his children. He frowns when dirty spirits are brought to the forefront; they are condemned. No man, woman, boy, or girl, is exempt from dishonest behavior. Committing intentional sin is against the law; and will be prosecuted.

Getting pregnant without following the principles of God's word, is intentional sin. Once the fetus is conceived, the connection will last lifelong. Once the baby is born, they are our responsibility. They have no knowledge of misbehaving; we must teach them how, to associate properly in society. We must put away our childish mindset and step up, as an mature loving parent. As the baby grow, they learn from what they see (another form of intentional sin).

EVIL SPIRITS

We must instill the spirit of God, at an early age, so they will adhere to authority, when they are older.

John 6:63 states, "It is the spirit who gives eternal life. Human effort accomplishes nothing, and the very words I have spoken to you are spirit and life."

Parents, as much as you don't want to admit, you are the reason why your children lack spiritual guidance **(intentional sin)**. There is a generational curse, that was passed down from those that came before you. Now, you have followed their pattern, and displayed disobedient behavior. You're to busy doing your own thing, and leaving the children to raise themselves. Then when they get in trouble, you want to put all the blame on them. That's false, you should put the blame on yourself, and the generations before you; you need proper parenting skills.

EVIL SPIRITS

Your behavior becomes erratic, and anger is taken out on the child; look in the mirror at the problem.

Look in the mirror and the problem will be revealed!

It's wrong for an adult to mistreat a child, that behavior is treacherous, deceitful, and immoral. We think we can take advantage of small people, but that is untrue; it causes abomination.

EVIL SPIRITS

When we deliberately attack them or others, whether physical or emotional, that is ruthless, wicked, and against the word of God. ***Will we get away with that evil spirit? The answer is, no?*** God is watching us, and as soon as we think we got away, the consequences will occur. I've been burnt by the fire of my struggles, hurt by the plagues of pain, and downtrodden by the mountain of pressures; yet, I'm still holding on to my sanity with God.

Without him, I can do nothing, and I am nothing. When devilish spirits try to weigh me down, I say, ***"with God I can do all things, through Christ who strengthens me."*** I've gone through many dark experiences, and I know for a fact, there is a true and living God. From the day I was born, until I was able to do for myself, I felt unappreciated. I lived in an abnormal situation that I didn't cause.

EVIL SPIRITS

I also encountered another disgraceful memory, I remember like it was yesterday. When I was in middle school, some uncontrollable boys, from my class, tried to gang up on me, in the hallway. Since, I was the last female to walk out, they felt the need to try and bully me. They laughed and caused a crowd to hover around, as they did a devilish act. I was touched inappropriately, and emotionally. I told them to leave me alone, but they continued.

My adrenaline kicked in, and they learned real quick, not to cross me with their nasty and cruel behavior. I lit into them, like a ticking time bomb, and when they saw, I wasn't weak, they ran away. I didn't let the get too far; I put scars on all of them. I got angry, because they had no right, to impose their unclean spirits on me. They mistreated other students, but they never got challenged; they made them cry.

Later that evening, we had a visit from the father of one of the boys; he was a police officer. Just so happened, my father was home when the officer arrived. He answered the door and welcomed them in, and asked what was going on. He told him, that I had bitten a chunk out of his son's chest. My father called me into the room, and asked me if I wounded the boy. My reply was, "yes, I hit, bit, and scratched him, and his bully friends."

I continued, "They tried to touch me inappropriately, and I told them to stop. They had a crowd, looking and laughing, and urging them to continue. After I saw, they were not listening, I used the tools you taught me, papa, to defend myself. I didn't want to hurt them, but they needed to stop being a bully." The boy's father asked his son if what I said was correct, as he held his head down, he said, "yes." The officer made his son apologize to me, and I was done.

EVIL SPIRITS

My father didn't punish me for protecting myself, he saw the anger, and frustration, as I spoke. Even though those boys didn't hit me, it was the act of trying to humiliate me. I refused to allow my peers to overstep my boundaries. So, you see, abuse followed me, from home to school; I didn't like the way I was treated. I tried to respect every one and look over their immorality, but that was not easy all the time. Those bullies never looked my way again, but I stayed ready just in case they did.

Through the abnormal occurrences, I learned how to see through my supernatural eyes; otherwise, I would have been confused. I talked to my heavenly father and asked him to make these insights clear. I said, "God, why did my peers choose me to pick on, and why did that lady choose me to treat cruelly? Please help me understand and make it through these tough situations."

EVIL SPIRITS

I just didn’t understand why I went through so much. As a child, I should have been happy and having fun, but my life was the exact opposite. I was humiliated with disrespect and felt like I had no self-worth. I enjoyed going to school, because it was a way of escaping the cruelty at home. So much evil was coming against me, but I'm glad God wouldn't allow me to self-destruct. Even though I was bruised inside, I still cherished my life.

I knew I wasn’t standing by myself, God was with me, all the way. He taught me how to stand bold during awkward times. The moments, I spent learning, I worshiped, and kept my mind calm, like the blue seas. I took advantage of his precious time, because I was safe in his arms, he never used or abused me. A brighter day came, when my peers saw me stand bold to the enemy; I fought the creep that jumped my brother.

EVIL SPIRITS

I did not allow any one to pick on him, I wasn't afraid anymore. Soon, the students wanted to join my circle, I became the representative for the less fortunate peers. I took up for the students that was talked down too, or bullied. I would be ready to tie one on, if they looked at me the wrong way. I knew how to defend the enemy, that caused, my friends, to be unhappy. Once I balled up my fist, the party was on; I didn't play with them.

People with evil spirits, do not treat individuals with kindness, and love; they're behavior is inhumane.

EVIL SPIRITS

To show you how evil spirits are, one day my friend and I, was about to leave school. I saw a brown bag, folded up in a bush, I looked closer and saw what appeared to be money hanging out. I showed them, and they got all excited. Suddenly, I heard, “get that money.” I hesitated for a moment, then with my trembling hands, I reached in and pulled it out.

My heart was pondering rapidly, with tears in my eyes, I didn't know what to do. I knew I was a child of God, and no matter what, I needed to do right. We went to the office, to turn the money in, and the person we saw was the clerk. She looked at me like, she hated me, and she had never seen me before. I handed her the bag, and said, “Ma'am I,” She immediately saw the money and started speaking real low. She said, “you're the one that stole my money.” My mouth flew wide open, after she accused me of stealing.

I guess she didn't think I heard her, so I gave her the bag, and she snatched it from my hand. She started counting the bills, and then said, “you stole some of it, there is only five-hundred dollars here, and fifty is missing.” I tried to tell her, I didn't steal anything, but she didn't listen. I had a thought, that came to mind, why was she almost whispering? I continued, “I found the money and turned it in right away.”

She kept frowning like she didn't believe me. When my friend saw how she was attacking me, she said, “she's telling the truth, we were together. When she saw the bag, she showed me, it looked like some money was hanging out. You're wrong to accuse her of stealing, and she found it, and brought it back.” The lady kept talking, very low, then threatened to call the cops. I said, “you don't have to believe me, God saw all of it, I'm not a thief.”

I continued, "and my father taught me better than that, I didn't even know how much was in the little bag." I then said, "Ma'am a bill fell out, and that's how I knew, money was in there; do you get it now? Somebody else stole your money, and by the way, like I said, I'm not a thief." She made me mad, and I walked out of the office.

"If God is for you, who can be against you."

I can't believe, I was accused of theft, and I was the righteous one. I learned, that no matter what we do, we are put in the same category as a criminal. That feeling was unpleasant, but I knew God had my back. I knew I did right, when I turned the money in, but the devil tried to make me look like I was a crook. If she had called the police, I would have been punished for the wrong reason.

EVIL SPIRITS

People treat us with disrespect because the world is full of detrimental sin; they have a lack of spirituality and no remorse. As I was leaving, the principal saw me, and said, “little girl, why are you crying?” I looked at him, and couldn't answer, I was so overwhelmed. My friend said, “Judy was accused of stealing, and that lady right there, treated her like a dog.”

She continued, “if she was a thief, she wouldn't have brought the money back. I'm glad I came in here with her, as a witness, because some grownups are messy.” I was surprised to hear my friend speaking up, she used to be quiet. I was always the verbal one, but my anger got the best of me. The principal said, “thank you, young lady, where did you find it?” My friend responded again, “Judy saw the bag in a bush, and it looked like money hanging out, so she got it and brought it to the office.”

EVIL SPIRITS

He said, "thank you so much, our painter reported that he lost some money. I know he will be so grateful, where is the money?" I looked at him funny because that clerk said it was her money. I said, "sir I gave it to the clerk." I thought about getting revenge, and telling him what else she said, but I kept quiet. I knew my battle had already been won; victory was mine. As the clerk handed over the money, she looked at me with hatred. I didn't care because she was wrong for lying. She knew that money didn't belong to her; she was the thief.

"When you know the right thing to do, just do it. Evil is always present to entice wrongdoings. God instilled in us, the gift of choices, and decisions. We can do good or bad.

~Author Judy C. Linzy

Just so happen, the painter was at the school, Principal Ed., called him to the office, right away. When he walked in and the money was handed to him, tears fell from his eyes. He said, “thank you so much, now I can pay my rent.” The principal said, “you are so welcome, but here are your guardian angels; they found the money.” The nice man rewarded us, and it was well appreciated. I looked at the clerk, and wanted to tell her off, but I knew God took care of her.

We gave the man a handshake and left. When we got outside, we counted our money, and my friend appeared to be sad. I said, “what's wrong Nodna?” She said, “I received more money than you, why did he do that? You should have received more, or the same amount.” She wanted to go back and say something, but I told her not too. I then explained to her, the reason why I thought she received more.

I said, "because, you stood up to that lying clerk, God saw the great thing you did." I wanted to make her feel good, so I remained positive. I also said, "you are a great friend, I'm alright with the money I received." Telling the truth, was worth more to me, than any amount of money. The Lord gave me wisdom, to handle this situation; he told me to always be honest.

I got past that situation and focused on my graduation day. I walked into my new blessing when I turned fourteen. I graduated, and enrolled into middle school, then I felt a breath of happiness.

"Knowledge is Power, it purifies the mind."

My feelings changed, when I had to go home. I learned how to fight the battles that continued to hinder me; I wanted to keep the peace.

EVIL SPIRITS

I was determined to not allow the enemy, to pull me down to his level.

"It is God who arms me with strength, and makes my way perfect. He makes my feet like the feet of deer and sets me on high places. He prepares me for battle; he strengthens me to draw a bow of bronze."

"He has given me the shield of his salvation, his right hand supports me, and his gentleness has made me great. He has made a wide path for my feet, to keep them from slipping. I chased my enemies and caught them; I did not stop until they were conquered."

"I struck them down so they could not get up; they fell beneath my feet. God, you armed me with strength for the battle; you subdued my enemies under my feet."

Psalm 18:32-39

I was excited to get the next school years started, so I could graduate again. This was the major step, and I wanted to make my dad proud.

EVIL SPIRITS

I studied hard and ignored the obstacles that followed me every day. That lady taunted me as a child, and continued to do so, when I became a teenager.

A steady flow of peace, will mend your broken heart!

I thought about telling my father so many times, but I kept quiet. I knew the perfect one to fight my battle. I said, "I lift my hands up to you my father; this battle is too much for me, but not for you." I felt great vibes, after I got rid of that nasty feeling. God took it, and I let it alone so he could work it out.

"No weapon formed against you shall prosper, and every tongue which rises against you in judgment, shall be condemned. This is the heritage of the servants of the Lord, and their righteousness is from me," says the Lord.

Isaiah 54:17

EVIL SPIRITS

I felt good because my father was so proud of me; I loved him so much. I wondered if he would feel the same, if I told him, his mate abused me, when I was a young girl. I didn't want to cause any unhappiness for him, so I chose to take her nasty attitude. I continued in school with a positive mindset, and tried to stay out of the woman's way. I wanted to talk to her, but I couldn't make the words come out of my mouth; she was cruel and mean.

I couldn't believe she hated me when I was born; what did I do to her? I couldn't answer that, but I knew my father in heaven would work it out. In the midst of that unpleasant thought, daddy came home. I went running and he made me feel much better. I asked him if he had time to talk, his reply was, "yes baby girl, always, let daddy get cleaned up and we'll have our conversation." I said, "okay daddy, I'll be right here, waiting."

After an hour, he said, "okay baby, what you want to talk about." I said, "graduation day is coming soon, and I'm excited; I wanted to make you proud of me." I then said, "are you proud of the young lady, I have blossomed into?" He said, "yes I'm very proud of you, you're my angel." I smiled, because that lady couldn't take my daddy from me. She was jealous and wanted him all to herself. Every time she looked at me, I saw hatred, and the looks of the devil. I knew she wanted to hit me, but she just frowned, with a balled-up fist. Quietly, I prayed for God to touch her, in a miraculous way.

"Violence is a behavior involving physical force, intended to hurt, damage, or kill someone of something."

I also wanted him, to show her how to love people, and then she would be loved back. I think she went through hard times; because she seemed so bitter. Maybe her parents didn't love her or maybe she was adopted. I quietly said, "maybe she got hurt real bad in another relationship; whatever the case may be, I didn't do it to her." After the talk with my father, I felt like a princess, I knew he loved me.

I went to my room and completed my homework; then I went to the senior center and helped them write letters. I was so happy, when I saw the smiles on their faces. I said, "God thank you for giving me the knowledge to help those in need, Amen." When I got back home, I thought about how fast my graduation date was approaching. I got sad because I didn't have anything to wear. My father paid all the bills, so I knew he didn't have money to buy me anything.

MOVES OF THE ENEMY

The lady caused many problems in our home, but daddy still kept her there. I didn't see any love between them, but I guess, love can be invisible. I thought love was showing action, not hurt and pain. I didn't agree with that at all, but that's what dad wanted. I looked in the drawer to put on my play clothes, and saw a pair of beautiful white flat heel shoes, and a pair of stockings. My mouth dropped wide open, in hopes of them being for me.

I thought they might had been for my graduation, but I wasn't sure. I pranced out the door to go play, and got bad looks from the woman. When I got back, I said, "Ms, how are you today?" I thought if I spoke to her, she would think differently about me. She looked at me, and flicked her hands, as if to tell me, to keep stepping. I thought that was mean and rude. I felt sad, so I went to my room.

I knew I was supposed to respect all adults, and more so, cause she was my daddy's mate. I said, "I guess she's had a hard life, and no spiritual connection." I went to my drawer and looked at those shoes again, and got happy. They were so pretty and I imagined myself wearing them. I figured they were bought for my little cousin, since she always got what she wanted.

My father hadn't mentioned to me, that he was going to buy me anything to wear; so I remained sad. The day of my graduation, I felt worse because I still didn't have any clothes to wear. All of a sudden he walked in, and saw me laying on my bed. He said, "my beautiful princess, get your shoes and stockings out of the drawer, and here's your dress; we have a graduation to attend." I looked at the dress and it was gorgeous. It was made of white chiffon pleated material, and a pretty lace down the front.

Everyone but the lady was excited to see my attire; they even helped me get ready. My aunt fixed my hair, into beautiful Shirley Temple curls. Once I was dressed, I felt like a shining star. Daddy said, "you're so beautiful," my chariot awaits you." It wasn't a horse and a buggy, but our ride was just as good. He held his hand out and escorted me to the car, then said, "my beautiful Princess Judy, this is your night, I'm so proud of you."

I felt like I was on top of the world, I was so happy. When we arrived, my father escorted me in, and all eyes, were on me; I was the queen of the night. I went to the area to get ready; because I had a surprise for daddy. For the first time, he heard me sing; I poured my heart into that song, and all I saw was his hands waving in the air. The entire night was perfect, I felt so good about myself, and I was treated with royalty.

Quietly I said, "God it's because of you, this night went so well. You are my savior, and no one will ever take your place." I told my father, how special he made me feel, and that I truly appreciated his love. I also told him, I was glad God gave me the best father, in the world. When we made it home, I thanked him again for an exuberant evening. As pretty as I felt, I didn't want to take the dress off.

I knew I had to go to school the next day, so I went to bed. I said, "God here I am again, I'm so happy, thank you; Amen!" I went to sleep and slept the whole night. When my clock went off, I still had the feeling of being a queen; my hair still had curls. When I walked into the school building, I received so many compliments, from the staff and students. I was showered with praises, and the students that tried to bully me, spoke nice to me.

I thanked all of them and went to my class. After school, I hurried home, so I could look at my beautiful attire again. I looked in the drawer and my shoes were gone; I knew that woman took them. She always stole everything my father bought for me. I thought about confronting her, but I knew God would fight that battle. I told him, I was tired of her behavior, and the time had come for me to tell my daddy.

I waited for him to get home and I said, "can I talk to you?" He said, "Sure baby, what's up?" I told him the way I had been treated by his partner, every since I was a young girl. I also told him, I didn't want to cause any trouble, so I kept it to myself. I looked at him, and his facial expression looked like he was about to cry. He told me not to worry, he would handle everything. Weeks passed, and the house was quiet, we stayed out of each other's way.

MOVES OF THE ENEMY

I didn't have any more problems out of her, she stayed in total silence. Supper time approached, and we gathered at the table. I wondered why she wasn't eating, then I saw her packing her suitcases to the door. I smiled because I knew a breakthrough was on the way; I smelled freedom in the air. Let her go and pick on someone else, I've had enough.

Minutes later, I heard a horn blow, it was a cab, there to pick her up. As she walked out, she seemed like she wanted to say something, but she turned and walked away. Once she left, I felt stronger and ready for a change. I began thinking, about my future, and how I could better myself. I was a growing girl, and needed many items, but I didn’t want to bother my father. I knew he had so much going on; I didn't want to add to it. I talked to God, and told him, If I had a sewing machine, I could make my clothes.

MOVES OF THE ENEMY

I was told, to always ask, and my wish would be granted. I felt alright, but I just didn't see it coming. One day, my dad came home early, and asked me if I wanted to go for a ride. I replied, "yes sir, where we going?" He said, "to visit your godfather." We traveled miles, and I must say, I felt good, being with my father. When we arrived, he got out and opened my door, and then said, "this is what a gentleman, is supposed to do, remember that."

My godfather, Jerry, greeted us and said, "come on in." We enjoyed our time, laughing and eating with him, and my godmother Jane. After a while he got up from the table and left the room. When he returned, he said, "Goddaughter, I got a question to ask you." I said, "tell me, tell me." He said, "my wife doesn't use her sewing machine anymore, do you want it?" I smiled and said, "oh my gosh, yes I do?"

I continued, “I want to learn how to make my clothes; thank you so much.” I was surprised, because I prayed to my heavenly father, about needing a machine. My wish was granted, and that made me a believer. When we got ready to leave, I kissed them and said I would visit again soon. The day I went, I wanted to surprise them, but I got a surprise. My godfather Jerry had passed away, and I didn't know he was sick.

I got sad because he didn't get to see me make my first piece of clothing. I was unhappy for a while, but after talking to my father, he made me understand about sickness and death. I told him, I would check on godmother Jane, since she was all alone. Every week I went and helped her with the household chores, she treated me with love. I thought of her like she was my mother. She was a beautiful and kind person, with a great spirit.

MOVES OF THE ENEMY

Weeks later, I thought about how nice it was, since my brother and I, had our father to ourselves; it was so peaceful. I went from being treated like nothing, to a young lady with dignity. One afternoon daddy came home and said, "let's go for a ride." I wanted to ask him where we were going, but I knew he wanted to surprise me. We pulled into the sewing shop, and he said, "surprise, this is your day, get everything you need."

I was totally surprised, so I got different color materials, patterns, thread, needles, etc. I didn't know anything about following a pattern, so I looked at my other clothes and followed that pattern. After that day I made all my clothes; I was so thankful. Months later, I surprised dad with a brand new work shirt, made by me: he was happy and appreciative. From that time on, I never had to buy clothes again, I also made several aprons for my Godmother.

MOVES OF THE ENEMY

I went to visit her and she was so happy when I gave her the aprons. She said, "thank you baby, you're so beautiful and talented." I felt so comfortable talking to her, she never criticized me. We talked about girly things, and boundaries, we are not to cross in life. I was growing up and knew my father wouldn't know how to answer questions, about female stuff.

Mama Jane, knew the exact words to say, and I felt so good. I finally had a mother figure, that I could love, and receive love. All the years, while I was young, I didn't know I had godparents. I guess he brought them into my life at the right time.

"God will supply our every need, according to his riches in glory, in Christ Jesus."

Philippians 4:19

MOVES OF THE ENEMY

In my last years of school, I didn't need any clothing, I was ready to complete my studies so I could graduate. I enrolled in a Home Economics class, to learn how to sew with a pattern. I was so happy cause I exceeded my level of understanding; my life was amazing. You see, all we have to do is ask and trust God, because he is the way. He may not come when we want Him, but He's always on time.

God is the only way we can cope with life, we must treasure every moment before it's too late. Our lives are torn apart when we face difficult situations. Sometimes, people stay in denial, instead of facing their state of condition. Just like my father's mate, she never dealt with her inner demons, and it destroyed her. She lost control because she didn't know how, and who to pray to. She must have thought aggression, anger, and revenge, was the way to solve her problems.

MOVES OF THE ENEMY

Looking back, I want to say to all adults, it's wrong to take advantage of small children. Mischievous, and secretive behavior is against God, you will reap what you sow. Abuse, is a cruel and violent treatment, towards a living being. That behavior is abnormal and is punishable by the law. Young children and animals can't defend themselves, they look up to us to love them. You will not get away with your devilish acts; you will suffer the consequences. Often, repercussions could last a long time, imprisonment is an option.

"Don't be misled, remember, you can't ignore God, and get away with it. You will always reap what you sow! Those who live only to satisfy their own sinful desires, will harvest the consequences of decay and death."

MOVES OF THE ENEMY

Adults think they can do what they want, and to who they want, but that is false. Disobeying the principles of God's word, is a sin.

"Those who live only to satisfy their sinful desires, will harvest the consequences of decay and death."

"Those who live to please the spirit will harvest everlasting life. Don't get tired of doing what is good, and don't get discouraged and give up. You will reap a harvest of blessings, at the appropriate time. Whenever we have the opportunity, we should do good to everyone, especially to our Christian brothers, sisters and our children." Life is how we treat it, good or bad!

MOVES OF THE ENEMY

Young children and animals can't defend themselves from the enemy, they look up to us to fight for them. I want you to listen to the cries of an abused child, have you witnessed it before?

"Please forgive me, don't hurt me anymore, please understand me! I'm sorry, please don't hit me no more; I thought you loved me! Stop, please stop; I can't take it! You're hurting me, I'll do whatever you say, just stop beating me!"

Does that sound familiar?

Adult tends to take their frustrations out on the children. They lose control and become emotional and hostile. They are wrong for taking advantage of a weak little person. Hitting on them with forceful aggression is against God.

MOVES OF THE ENEMY

When I was going through harmful times, I talked to God from my heart. I felt like I had no one else tangible that would listen to me. All kinds of evil went through my head, but I chose to let God fight my battles. When children go through harmful times, they develop hurt, pain, and emotional scars. They also experience fear, shame, loneliness, and suicidal thoughts. They feel withdrawn, and not worthy of being in society; they become emotionally trapped.

The mind is a powerful tool, it can portray good or evil. You must clear your mind of all negative thinking; so you can make positive changes. Negativity causes destruction (**tearing apart**), you get stuck in one place. You will never know God's plan if you're not free to move. Positive tendencies causes construction (**putting together)**. It's better when our life is linked together, rather than shattered apart.

Parents that possess spiritual knowledge, and obedience, will teach their children the proper way. So when they get older, they will not depart from it. If they do fall, they will have the strength to get back up.

~Judy C. Linzy

I thought about the time when I was put on a nerve medication called Red Devil. It made me feel like I was in a trance, my head was spinning. I couldn't understand why I had to take that stuff, at a young age. It gave me an uncomfortable feeling, and I dealt with abnormal conditions. I suffered from drowsiness, lack of energy, and wild thoughts. Often, when I fell asleep, I saw a big red devil with pointed ears and a long tail, standing by my bed. I woke up in fear and breathing hard; that stuff caused me to have weird dreams.

It caused me, to not have proper control, of my character. I couldn't believe the doctor would prescribe such powerful medication. During that horrible experience, I was asked to babysit for a single mother. I loved children, I volunteered any time I could. I took care of the child, just like she was my own.

The time came, for me to take that horrible medicine, I immediately went to bed. I got sleepy, so I put the baby girl, right next to me. I slept a while, but when I woke up, she wasn't there. My heart started beating fast, so I jumped up and went looking for her. I went to the other rooms, but I still couldn't find her. I got nervous because I knew my world, was about to crash. My mind told me, to look under the bed, and there she was, sound asleep. When that mean lady, saw me looking for her, the next day, after my father went to work, I was punished.

She grabbed me by my hair, and locked me in a small dark cramped closet, for two hours. She didn't care that it had no ventilation, nor standing room. When the child's mother came to pick her up, the lady told her so many false stories, and she became furious. I didn't get to babysit anymore; I was sad.

I became angry because that woman said bad things about me, it made me look like an unfit sitter. I believe she was the one, that removed the baby from the bed. She knew how the medication would affect me. My father had no idea, that she threw me in that closet. I didn't want to tell him, cause I knew she would lie. When I got older, I saw all the unearthly acts, that were thrown at me. I think she was jealous of my father, and my relationship. Plus, she hated me, because I would not call her, my step-mother; I only had one mother.

I also believe, she was the reason, I had to take that horrible drug. I asked God to show me if she was the enemy. When I was finally released from it, I felt exhausted and became hostile; I was unable to think clearly. My emotions became unhealthy and my mind started to unravel. Rage came upon me, and I wanted to destroy the grown-ups that abused me.

I looked at myself as unworthy, and ugly. The hostility I incurred, caused a detrimental effect. That woman destroyed my happiness, and I was torn down, with nothing but sadness. I felt so dark inside, my life was meaningless. I said, "I will get rid of them, one at a time." I became bitter, had low self-esteem, and no one could tell me anything. I must say, I'm so thankful, God stepped in and blocked the activity of that situation. I give all praises unto him because the evil spirit was trying to destroy his child.

"I developed so much hatred, I was emotionally sick."

I'm so grateful it was only a close call; my life got back on track. No one knew the hurt I went through, but God did. That was the consequence, for me not knowing, how to deal with the root, of my problems. The wicked evil of darkness tried to overpower, and inject me, with destructive thoughts. I had a feeling of bitterness, rejection, fear, and more. I thought I knew it all, only to find out, I was setting myself up for failure. I paid more attention to the devilish acts, of the wicked people, but I should have listened to my heavenly father. I learned, that when it seems as though something or someone, is trying to block us, we must pray until something happens **(push)**.

"I got extremely angry because I should have known better."

MOVES OF THE ENEMY

The closer, we get to the connection of God, we will experience, the freedom from within. Our life will blossom, our light will shine, and give off an array of brightness. We must forgive the people, we feel have treated us wrong, so your life can be transformed, into a positive success. We must not allow bad thoughts, to live in our minds; it is toxic. I decided to show love, instead of just saying it; it is an action word, and it conquerors all things. When we learn to love, everything else will follow.

"You always gain by giving love; where there is love, there is life. Never give up, when there is a godly potential."

Reese Witherspoon

MOVES OF THE ENEMY

John 3:16 - God so loved the world, he gave His only begotten Son, that whosoever believes in him will not perish, but have everlasting life.

The question is, **"are we hurting other than ourselves when we choose not to love and forgive others?"** Ex., If we fall and puncture our lungs, we will not breathe properly, eventually, we will expire, if there is no repairable treatment. The same thing, if we don't forgive others, it will slowly deteriorate our mind, then kill us.

Forgiveness is a yoke of bondage, that allows our mind to be set free, not only for the forgiven but to release the forgiver. We have a tendency, of tying a noose around our neck, by wrong thinking. Don't bottle your anger, and resentments inside of you.

Don't let the enemy kill you!

MOVES OF THE ENEMY

Bitterness will set in, and a valley of dry bones shall occur; don't be your own worse enemy. Rise above hurting situations, and allow the spirit of God, to flourish within you; the darkness will then flee. Being stuck in a dark place, is an unearthly curse, of the enemy. Your soul will be blocked from living, you will feel like you're chained and imprisoned.

God's powerful anointing, will enable you to become successful and fly like an eagle. As an adult, we must learn how to depend on his favor and blessings. As a child, there is no knowledge; your job is to teach them. However, you can't teach them until you've been taught. Generations that have gone on before us, have caused a detrimental curse upon our children. Some adults still live in the past, with no hopes for the future. Children also have a fear of learning, when domination and intimidation, occur.

MOVES OF THE ENEMY

Parents, guardians, adults; let's rise above the detriments of life. Children should always feel secure, and comfortable, talking to us. Show them, you're a caring person, and they don't have to hide from you. Assure them, they have the right to convey information without any repercussion. Show them at an early age, that they can trust and confide in you. Let them know, they have the right to speak freely, about what they're feeling. Our duty as parents is to listen and offer helpful solutions.

"You are their first point of contact, and if you show no concern, they will turn to whomever they feel will listen; the decision of that behavior could be unhealthy."

Parents my advice is to, **"let it be you, that they talk to; otherwise, they will turn to someone else. That is not a great idea, the outcome could be harmful."**

If they require professional therapy, be by their side; learning could help both of you. Be careful who you go to; they must be caring adults as well. They must have the ability to listen, with an attentive heart. Pay close attention to your child's facial expression, it could tell a different story. If there is a conflict between parent and child, then you may have to observe from another setting.

Abuse is a widespread epidemic, and as for children, it is our job to protect them. The problem I see; we get so wrapped up, in our own filthy messed up lives, we neglect their needs. Then, they are vulnerable in the hands of an abuser. We lose focus of our priorities and show attention towards the unethical perpetrator. Children should not have to suffer from our selfish and immoral behavior. It's our fault when we get into unhealthy relationships; we have power.

MOVES OF THE ENEMY

We keep our hearts and mind, on the attacker, thinking our love will change them. Then we become mentally bogged down, trying to make them happy. Our children will suffer from a lack of nurturing and attention. If someone abuses you, they will surely do the same to your children; with a stronger dominant force. Abuse is against the word of God, and punishable by the law.

Some parents have silenced their children from telling the truth, to benefit themselves. They rather live with immoral behavior, than to follow the principles. Teaching them to lie is unethical and inhumane, they do not deserve that treatment. They become confused, especially, when they are chastised, for doing, what you told them to do.

Let me ask this question, "parents, do you think you're right?

Why do you feel, you have the right, to make your children tell lies, because of what you're doing, in front of them?" Your selfishness is more important than your child's mentality or safety?

A predator could be lurking behind the closed door, waiting for the perfect time to strike you or your children.

BEHIND THE CLOSED DOOR

This is a journey no one should want to travel – Beware! I know you see, how destroyed the world is, our children can't play outside anymore. Evil spirits are hidden, watching and waiting, to deter them from reality. Parents, it's your job to protect your children. Be aware of who you accept into your home, your children's life depends on you.

"Don't trust anyone, because you think you know them, or associate with them; they may be in disguise. Trusting them with your precious jewels (your children), is the ingredients for disaster. An abuser does not have a heart, they target the weak and confused."

These days, some family members, can not be trusted. Pay close attention to their shifty eyes and sneaky behavior.

BEHIND THE CLOSED DOOR

At the young age of five, I was sexually molested by a teenage family member, of my father's mate. Dad was a remarkable man and helped anyone he could. He allowed the homeless boy to stay for a few weeks. He gave him a job, so he could get up on his feet. It's okay to have the compassion to help others, but some people are not genuine. The seventeen-year-old, was put in the same room with my brother and me; my daddy believed in him and wanted to help.

Late one night, as soon as I fell asleep, I felt heavy breathing in my ear. I opened my eyes, and he was standing over me in the dark, whispering obscene words. I was about to holler, but he covered my mouth. I didn't know what was happening, fear set in, and I panicked. I'm so thankful, he didn't get the opportunity to rape me, but I was petrified. **"Never trust people that look sneaky."**

Imagine a huge man standing over you or your child, in the dark. The thought of that was devastating and scary. Right after the incident, I started hollering and crying. My brother woke up and asked me what was wrong, I told him what happened, so he went running, to get my father. Daddy came right away, and soon as he saw me, he knew something was wrong. He asked me what happened, and after I told him, he immediately threw the boy out.

I looked at the woman's face, and all I can say, "if looks could kill." I didn't have respect or rights, when I was a little girl, but my prayers took care of the problem. That's why it is so important, to let parents know, the importance of securing their children's safety. That boy was a predator, he secretly watched me, and when the time was right, he took advantage. A predator is a sneaky scoundrel, waiting to attack -**Beware!**

Also be aware of your friends, that come to visit, ask to use the bathroom, and stay gone for a long time. They could be checking out where your children sleep. Also, pay close attention to babysitters and friends, of your friends. The evil spirit comes around when you least expect it. Your child is innocent and does not deserve the trauma of being violated. A sexual molester, is a ruthless hunter, that prey on individuals, that are vulnerable or fearful. He does not care who his victim is, no one is exempt. He will strike when he thinks the time is right.

Predators hang out at playgrounds, waiting to snatch your small child.

The sneaky crooked eye monster, could be watching your child while he/she sleeps. When he thinks the time is right, he will abuse the helpless child. The rapist could cause a traumatic detriment, and /or death. Parents beware of the people you invite into your home; they may not be trustworthy.

The nasty beast will preferably make his move at night or in secluded areas. Parents, young children are not equipped, with the knowledge, to defend themselves. An adult is to dominate for a small child. Pay close attention, and do not let them out of your sight, when they're playing. Also, do not let them go to public restrooms, by themselves; that is dangerous. Parents remember, sexual abuse, is the result of abusive behavior, that takes advantage of a child's vulnerability.

“Perpetrators look for passive, quiet, troubled, and lonely children.”

Once your child's little life has been violated, it affects their functional abilities. They become confused, and abnormal acting; then they shutdown from reality. The effects can be devastating, because they feel betrayed and unable to trust adults.

"Abuse is a traumatizing experience, especially for a young child."

~Judy C. Linzy

An Evil spirit could presents himself as a person that is in need of help. Often, his head is held down to shield his identity, and when the time is right he will strike – Beware!

The behavior of the devil, comes through the people you interact with everyday – Beware, they could be putting on an act!

A Sexual Predator looks normal and innocent – Beware!

"Do not allow the enemy to kill, steal, and destroy your conscience."

Adults, let's talk about **R-E-S-P-E-C-T for your children,** it is an action word, and for it to be received, it must be shown. You must present yourself in an mature adult manner and your children will learn the proper way. Teach them the ***Fruits of the Spirit***, and both you will be rewarded. There will be an abundance of joy, love, peace, happiness, and the greatness of God's word. Respect is also gained by what we do and how we act. We will not receive it, until we give it, so take note:

1. Listen to what they have to say, do not cut in when they are talking.

2. Show kindness towards them, make them feel important, and treat them the way you want to be treated.

Children deserve Respect too!

I was disrespected as a child, but as I got older, I learned some valuable information. People hurt people, because they hurt, and want everybody to feel their pain. Also, they could have been, abused and neglected, in their childhood. They were not raised to love, so when they became an adult, they had the same mentality, it was passed on from past generations.

"My body had many scars, but God turned them into stars. He does not look at the outer condition, he focuses on the inside of our soul. He gave me beauty for ashes, and now I can smile with joy."

~Judy C. Linzy

I'm so glad the world didn't give me this smile, and that lets me know, they can not take it away.

I learned, that the joy of the Lord is my strength. What the enemy meant for harm, God turned it around. I didn't trust adults, so I had no one to talk to. I only felt comfortable, talking to my heavenly Father. I knew he loved me, and would never harm, hurt, or throw me in a dark closet. I prayed to him and said, **"Father when I grow up, please don't let me be rude, aggressive, and destructive towards another human being; especially children."**

"Give me the strength to stand firm and cherish them, teach me to be a good listener." I also said, **"when I become an adult, I want you to send me a husband that will love and cherish me, like you do, Amen."**

Children should not be afraid to express their thoughts and feelings. Show them you love them, and will always provide the best care.

Once they see and feel that, a bond will be established, and the relationship will become sacred. When individuals, especially children, are victimized, like I was, it is very traumatic. I was abused at an early age, and didn't have the opportunity to receive proper nurturing, love and guidance. I knew my father loved me, but he worked all the time.

"Children must be loved, so they can learn how to love."

Just to think, about me not having my mother to bond with, was a feeling, some, would not understand. I cried out to God many days and nights for clarification, about what happened. He led me to see, as I matured, I would understand the concepts of life. I must say it took a while, but I did see, what is often said, "the big picture." God showed me, my experience, would be a blessing to others, that may have encountered the same struggle.

I also remembered the prayer, I said to God. I asked him to grant me with the proper character and the ***Fruits of the Spirit.*** I said, **"God, please let me grow up treating people the way I want to be treated. Do not allow my character to fall beneath, being godly. Also if I am granted with a husband, that has children, please, make sure I love them, as if they were my own."**

"Don't let my past control my future; let me possess the Fruits of the Spirits. I want to teach them the utmost values and qualities of life." Then I said, **"I won't demand them to call me, "stepmother," unless they want too. Help me Lord to be a model of you, I don't ever want them to feel what I've felt, Amen."**

The big day came, when I married my first love, I then became a mother, and my life changed. Due to conflicting values, our union disconnected, and we divorced.

Years later, I was blessed with the man I prayed for. He had Christian morals, values, and standards. We got married and started our journey with his children and mine. I nurtured all of them the same and made sure their needs were met. We lived in the ways of the Lord, and that made life easier. I was so grateful, God gave me exactly what I prayed for.

Suddenly I had thoughts of my childhood, I lived with many trials, tribulations, and troubles. I cried to God about the evil spirits, that kept stirring up, devilish acts, in our home. I always went to my comfort areas, to pray, I knelt down on rocks, chicken corn, and even rice. My knees were hurt to the core, but I knew the pain in my heart, was worse. God told me to ask and my desires would be granted. I gained enough strength, to resist the behavior of the adults, that mistreated me.

He taught me, how to endure the pain; because there is power, after an emotional experience. I am most grateful, he stood with me, and showed me a better way. He didn't condemn, abuse, or take advantage of me, for making mistakes.

"My Savior is my life."

He knew, I would learn how to live right, as I continued my walk with him. My heavenly Father told me to depend on him, for my strength. He also told me, my father on earth, would take care of my brother and me, until we became adults. After then, he would take over, and provide direction. He also said, if we disobeyed his principles, we would get chastised.

I am so grateful, that I at least, had my earthly father, to love and lean on; when I was a child. He had the same loving character as God.

After the demon was removed, my father seemed to smile more, He took us to church, and told us how must he appreciated us. I knew he wasn't happy with that woman. I felt so good, to be serving God with my daddy. Being there gave me a feeling of comfort, and I knew his presence, stood beside me. I heard his voice, just like he, was in front of me. He said, "I have the power to change negative to positive; walk with me."

I must say, even though daddy worked all the time, when I was small, he was a wonderful role model. I wanted to follow in his footsteps because he taught us how to respect our elders. We had to say, "yes ma'am, no ma'am, yes sir, no sir, and thank you." I believe that's why I was taken advantage of; my kindness was taken for weakness. I was polite, but I was treated in a derogatory way.

The world saw me differently, as if I was nothing. I continued to follow my spiritual journey, that was my lifelong goal.

"Parents, listen to you children, they are not always wrong. Talk to them and get an clear understanding, before making a harsh decision."

~Discipline does not have to be forceful.

I also remembered, the good times we had, when my father gathered us on the porch, and listened to music. The neighbors joined us, and we started singing. Every Sunday, we sounded like a choir; we lit up the street. Sometimes I even listened to the radio all night; it relaxed my mind. Living in the home with demonic spirits, was frightening, but I learned how to overcome the negative experiences.

I prayed, and developed my spiritual way. So you see, my upbringing had a negative impact, but I was delivered by God's word. I listened to the directives of my father; I had to kind and caring. I struggled in that area, because the enemy kept hindering me. I was tired of the inhumane treatment, so my attitude changed. I immediately turned angry when I was approached, without the proper manner.

"Praise is another way of escape"

I didn't like to be disrespected, when I knew I told the truth. I was always brought down and accused of lying; that was not right. My father's mate continued her disobedient behavior; I couldn't stand the sight of her. I didn't say anything, but I sure wanted to. Instead, I cried out to God, who told me, to not do evil for evil. At the time, I didn't agree, because she wasn't hurting, I was.

I wanted to make her pain just as I did, then I thought about revenge. I knew I would receive a harsh penalty for my actions. I could possibly receive, double punishment, cause I knew better. My earthly father and my heavenly Father would inflict sever pain upon me. I know you're wondering how I could sing, and praise, when I was being accused of faulty accusations.

I did it in silence, my mouth was closed, and my mind was open and angry. When I got alone, I immediately spoke loudly to the Lord; it was just me and him.

"I spoke from my heart, as tears poured from my eyes, then I received my biblical nugget (my privileges in Jesus Christ)."

Suddenly I felt relief, something came over me. From that point on, I had a beautiful relationship with my Lord and Savior.

I received the right to life, and I was granted, to only associate, with a particular group of people. God gave me the privilege to always be with him, and stand proud of who I was. I also learned, anger, is the work of the enemy; blurting out without thought, could cause a detrimental catastrophe. I tried to obey everything he said, but it was very hard. I quietly said, "God must be testing my obedience, to see if I'm going to abide by the principles of his word."

"I beseech you therefore, brethren, by the mercies of God, that ye present your bodies a living sacrifice, holy, acceptable unto God, which is your reasonable service. And be not conformed to this world: but be ye transformed by the renewing of your mind, that ye may prove what is that good, and acceptable, and perfect, will of God."

Romans 12:1-2

Golden Nuggets.

1. **"For God so loved the world that he gave His one and only Son, that whoever believes in Him shall not perish but have eternal life." (John 3:16)**
2. **"And it shall come to pass, that everyone who calls on the name of the Lord shall be saved." (Acts 2:21)**
3. **"That if you confess with your mouth the Lord Jesus and believe in your heart that God has raised Him from the dead, you will be saved." (Romans 10:9)**

There are many more; better known as scriptures, and can be found in the **Bible**. After studying them, I learned to never speak abruptly and to always think before saying the first words.

One evening, I heard my father's mate say, my brother and I was bad, and she should send us to a home, for those type of children. I listened to what God told me not to do, so I held that negative feeling in my head. I prayed but it wouldn't go away, I started crying as I mentioned it to my brother. I told him what she said, and once again, I let the enemy take control; she caused me extreme anger.

I made the decision, I had, had enough, of the verbal, physical, and mental abuse. I told him what I was going to do, and for him to come with me. I didn’t want him to stay in that complicated situation; he needed to be free. At first, he agreed, but for whatever reason, he changed his mind. I was determined to do things my way, so I got my clothes and didn't think about me babysitting. I left the child with him and ran away.

I went out the back way, so that lady couldn't see me. I was tired of her mean and ugly behavior and wasn't taking it anymore. As soon as I was out of sight, I hollered:

"God, I just can't take this no more!"

I figured running away would be the solution to this tiresome troubled time. I was mentally anguished and didn't deserve the cruelty, that I had received. All I wanted, was, for the pain to go away, so I could live. I knew I would hurt my father but I overlooked that. I also knew when he got home and didn't see me, he would be concerned.

If he asked my brother, then he would tell him what I did. Daddy would come looking for me, and realize something had to be wrong. After I walked so far, I rested in a sugar cane field; the bugs were terrible. I felt uncomfortable and kept looking at the ground for snakes.

Then I thought about, being attacked by a wild animal, but I didn't want to go back to that abuse. I knew I was wrong, but I needed a way out. I decided to look out, and I got happy because I saw my dad's car coming. As it got closer, I came out of hiding; I was four miles down the road. He stopped, and said, “baby, get in.” I was still crying and relieved when I saw he was by himself. In my mind, I said, “thank you, God.”

I got in the car, and the ride back home was in silence. I didn't know how he would respond, but I knew, it was a perfect time, for me to tell him, what had been going on. Then he said, “why did you leave home?” I hesitated for a moment, then I told him, what his mate said. He didn't say anything back, but I knew he was listening. I guess he started analyzing what was happening, because the abused slowed down. I knew I was disobeying, but I needed a way out.

Soon afterward, the troubled woman moved out. She told on herself, but if he had paid closer attention, he would have known much sooner. My prayer was answered, daddy found out the truth for himself. I thank God, that he caught her in the act, everything that was done in the dark, came to the light. Heavenly Father was in the midst, even though I ran away; my behavior was wrong.

The decision I made, was very dangerous, and even more dangerous in this current time, I learned a valuable lesson:

"NEVER EVER run away from your problems."

Talk to God about anything that hinders you, and let him work it out. I promise you, he will give you a safe way to escape. One thing I know, my dad corrected me with love and I loved him too; he never abused me.

I promised my heavenly father, I would never allow anyone, to abuse me again, Through all my trials, tribulations, and troubles, I learned, two wrongs don't make a right. Instead of me talking, I put action to the evil spirit. People with that type of heart, love hurting others; they will never win. We must rise above them, and allow God to mend whatever is ailing us; he will heal our broken heart.

We must be strong and take the bitter with the sweet. I'm not saying, put yourself in a position to be abused, I'm saying to endure every hurt, and pain, and growth will develop. As we continue our walk in life, we realize, there is nothing we can do, without leaning on our heavenly father. He is the only one, who can keep us on track. We will always experience ill feelings, in some form or another, that's why we must stay connected, to our power source.

He will give us what we need to overcome negative setbacks. No matter how much abuse, I went through, or what thoughts I suffered from, I stayed focused on the master. I refused to let anything or anybody, interfere in my moving forward. Today, I'm so grateful for all the downfalls, I received, I learned how to live a prosperous life. Even though my brother and I, were raised by one parent, he taught us well; we were never mistreated by him.

In my first year of high school, my independence set in; my attitude change, and I started hanging with the wrong crowd. I got rebellious and my father had to discipline me. He made me write three-hundred to five-hundred lines; that was not a good feeling. Because of my disobedience, I had to repeat the ninth grade; my consequences taught me a lesson. I got tired of writing, the same thing over and over.

"Did my father discipline me for repeating the ninth grade?"

No, I disciplined myself the whole summer, I realized, I hurt him. I let myself down too; I knew I was wrong. God spoke to me and gave me a clear understanding of my mistakes. He showed me what I needed to do, to excel from the behavior. I followed his lead, and I felt myself growing. My mind started maturing with my body, and I took my responsibilities, seriously.

I expressed myself properly and handled my failures differently. I stood above the filth and learned how to act in a manner of greatness. I knew I had to abide by the principles of my Lord and Savior. With discipline, comes an abundance of strength, knowledge, and understanding.

I remember having an attitude with my male teachers. I did not adhere to their authority because they sounded like my father's mate. During that time, I developed a negative attitude. I didn't realize until later, that they could have had a positive impact on my education. My disobedience caused me to fail and that's why I had to repeat the course.

"Do not allow your attitude, and a lack of comprehension, to cause major setbacks."

If you need help, don't hesitate to ask, the teacher is there to make sure there is a clear understanding of the subject; ask questions. When we develop a teachable spirit, we become more precise and mentally capable.

"God will lead and guide you in all truths."

Psalm 31:3

Don't blame anyone for your evil spirits, **look in the mirror and see the real problem**; I did.

The problem is in the mirror, do you see the in-ner me (enemy)?

Holding on to obstacles, that weighed you down, a long time ago, will only hurt you. When you feel like everyone, has treated you wrong, you must turn to our heavenly Father, for comfort.

"You can do all things through Christ who strengthens you."

Philippians 4:13.

In the next school term, I mastered the two subjects and passed the classes. You see, I changed my attitude, towards, learning from male teachers. I did well for a while, then here I go again, another male teacher, causing me problems. Would you believe, I had to repeat that subject? I was having a hard time getting through my assignment because I didn't want to ask him for help.

As I sat in class, I had a frown, because I just didn't understand the assignment. One of the students that thought she was much smarter, than me, asked me, was I having problems. My response was, "yes." She then said, "I don't understand it either, so I'm not going to study anymore." I said, "well if you don't, you will get a bad grade."

She said, “I might have to copy off somebody's paper.” She also said, “Judy, I've never seen you copying off of no one.” I looked at her strangely and kept quiet. I said to myself, “why would I copy, I would be the one to get caught?” She then said, “I don't have time for this.” My eyes, bucked wide open because I thought she was so smart. Right then I learned another lesson, she was no better than me. I responded, “if you don’t study, you’ll have to repeat the course.”

I also said, “I'm going to study, so I can pass.” She asked me if I would help her, and I said, “yes, I sure will, let's study together.” So, I gave up my free time, and drilled her until she memorized the order of the first sixteen United States presidents; we both passed and graduated.

“The struggle got real”

My disobedience, set in again when I turned nineteen, I tried to hide all my problems, once again. I was faced with more trials, tribulations, and troubles. My mind was going in all directions, and all I thought about was negative stuff. I didn't talk to God like I was supposed to; I wasn't thinking about that. I took a hand full of pain relievers; thinking that would take care of my problem.

I wasn't ready to die, I just wanted some relief. My father came home at the right time and knew something was wrong. He saw how strange I was acting, and asked me what was wrong. I started crying and almost let the enemy keep my mouth shut. I didn't want to tell him, what I did. Something came over me and I said, “I took a hand full of pills, I'm tired of the pain.” I couldn't keep my eyes open, so he rushed me to the hospital.

As soon as I got there, my stomach was pumped until everything was spewed up. The doctors told him, I was lucky and got there just in time. My father sent me to counseling, and eventually, I felt much better. Everything I learned, allowed me to think clearly, and make wise choices.

"WARNING - NEVER play with these kinds of thoughts, or attempt to do dangerous acts, ask God to take away your evil thinking."

~Judy C. Linzy

My advice is to never play with your life; it causes a domino effect on your love ones. Not knowing, this was an act of playing with my life, but I soon learned consequences came very harsh, from being disobedient.

"When we hurt, they hurt."

I FOLLOWED THE LIGHT, BUT...

Chap. V

Think before you act, If you feel something is not right, don't proceed with it. God gives us an inkling, to know whether our decisions are right or wrong. We have to put our unearthly behavior away; it is from the pit of hell. We learn as a child, what we should and should not do. As we continue learning the proper provisions for our lives, we know what is best for us. Often, we do what we see others do, but we are lead down the wrong path. Then we want to get mad and hate the person, forever; it was our decision.

At an early age, my earthly father would always say, "no Judy, don't do that," or even, "you know you were wrong." Then he also said, "yes, you were right, you will always be rewarded for doing right Judy, do you understand now?"

Remember, right = rewards, and wrong = harsh penalties.

"Consequences last a long time!"

Now that we are adults, we must rely on our heavenly Father to steer us right. There is no other way, we can not live without him, we will fail. My father told me when I got grown, God would become my parent. I know, we think we have no authority over us, that is far from the truth. Just because no one is standing in front of us, God lives within.

We must listen and obey his principles, and we will do well. He has a plan, that we must adhere to, if we don't, we will suffer the consequences. I thank God for allowing me the opportunity to learn from my mistakes, and for placing a teachable spirit in me. If I wouldn't have corrected my attitude, my life would have been stifled, with no education.

There are so many people, that are still emotionally discouraged, and tormented by the problems in their lives. They are mentally damaged and feel like there is no hope.

"God kept my mind, and allowed me to hold on to my sanity."

He was there all the time, he wouldn't allow me to give up. We must remember, our decisions affect our family; positive actions, equal rewards, and negative, will result in detrimental repercussions.

There are repercussions for bad, and rewards for good!

Always think and pray before anything is said or done; make sure the maker is driving the ship. He will show you the way, when there seems to be a dead end. He was there through my many trials, and it remains the same today. After I mastered the counseling trauma, I had more freedom to think and associate on a higher level.

"Thank you, God for the many lessons you taught me. I know I was disobedient, but you never gave up on me."

I started doing well, then the enemy showed up again. I was on my way to the store, when a man in a truck, drove slow and stopped. He started talking to me real nice, then he said, "hea young lady, would you like to make some big money?" I looked at him and immediately thought, he was a predator.

I immediately responded, "No!"

That was the last straw, I knew I needed to do something different. I signed up for the Job Corps and got accepted. The only thing was, it was in another state, but I went anyway.

I FOLLOWED THE LIGHT, BUT...

When I arrived, I knew I was about to spread my wings, cause I felt grown. I settled in and realized the atmosphere, wasn't what I was used too. So all I did was read my books; I wanted to graduate and get out of there. My roommates invited me to go to activities with them, at first, I was undecided, but there was nothing else to do, so I went. I also noticed, one thing was missing, there were no spiritual services, no one worshiped at all.

Even though I seemed happy, I wasn't; the people I connected with, was the opposite of me. They tried to connect with me, but I was miserable, and couldn't think straight; my mind was twisted.

"I felt like a fish out of water."

I studied and tried to keep up with the nursing program, but I didn't do too well. I just couldn't keep my mind on it.

I FOLLOWED THE LIGHT, BUT...

After a while, I finally finished the program, and returned home. I was excited because I accomplished something. I knew I needed to keep moving forward, so I decided to test for the army. I didn't do great there either, I failed. I didn't stop, I took the test to enroll in college, but I failed it too. I then thought, the navy was another choice , so I signed up. The day of my physical, I found out I was pregnant.

At that point, I got discouraged and lost all thoughts, and the desire to succeed. I felt down and out, and didn't call on my strength maker, anymore. I decided to handle my problems. I knew being pregnant, would change my life forever.

"My life became disastrous, with no spiritual connection; I was disobedient, once again."

I got married, and thought I had found my soulmate; I wanted my bed of roses. After I had my baby, problems began; verbal and physical abuse. I lived with detrimental harm, but I rolled with the punches, cause I knew how to fight. I promised God, I would never allow anybody to abuse me again.

"Pay close attention, because the enemy sets up roadblocks."

After seven years, of trying to hold on to a ragged edge marriage, I decided to take my children and flee. I threw some clothes in my car, and never looked back. I moved in with relatives, which caused a lot of mental turmoil. The environment was not good, and I knew I wouldn't be there too long. There were too many people under the same roof. I needed to stay until my divorce was final, so we would have some kind of stability. If everyone had provided their own, the stay would have been alright.

I went days without eating, making sure my children didn't go hungry. I had very little money and didn't know where any more would come from.

"Never put your children in a situation that could result in a crime."

My mind told me to go to the Post Office, but I didn't see a reason, to walk that far. My car was down, and we were stuck in a bad situation. I tried to forget about the long trip, but the thought kept repeating. I wanted to ask for a ride, but no one at the house had transportation. I decided to take my children and walk to those long miles, just to see if my mind was right. We walked in the heat of the day, to the nearest town. When we got there, I was tired and exhausted. I asked the employee if I had any mail, and she gave me several letters.

To my surprise, I had two checks, I got happy, and suddenly, I wasn't tired anymore. I knew the space where I lived was overcrowded, and my children weren't happy. I immediately went to the store and cashed them. I got a cab to take us back to the house, and I immediately got my car fixed. We moved into our spot, and I felt free and ready to live. I started getting my head back together, cause I moved near a church.

My children and I started attending, and things got much better. God showed me the proper provisions, and I took each step. I got a job, enrolled my son in school, and my baby girl in daycare. I worked every day, and all I thought about, was picking my babies up and going home. On my off days, we attended church, and I felt my spiritual house, getting back in order. I started believing in the word of God, again.

The crooked line I used to walk, began straightening out, and I saw the light again. I said, **"Father, show me again, I'm all yours."** It's our choice to walk the proper line; we have all the power. I got stronger in my faith, belief, and hope; then I followed the principles of God's word. The choices we make, determine our strength and disobedience.

It will show how, and if, we will respond to our situations, in a positive way. When I was a child, I thought I was talking to myself, but I was actually communicating with God. I said, **"Father, thank you for lending me your ear, I know you will listen. You hear and understand, what I'm saying, and I trust you, Amen."** He will give us the strength to resolve our challenges. We must develop a prayer life with Him, so he can give you the required power to cross over each hurdle.

<u>Faith</u> provides hope, belief, and strength.

Each of them, could have a different affect, it may be simple or challenging. The difficulties I experienced as a child, prepared me for my adult life. It developed me in prayer, patience, and poise. The difficulties I experienced as a child, prepared me for my adult life.

"My challenges caused me weariness and anxiety."

The difficulties I experienced as a child, prepared me for my adult life. It developed me in prayer, patience, and poise. My life got easier after every challenge, I overcame. Believe it or not, struggles were formed, when we were inside our mother's womb. God created a passageway, for us to learn survival skills. We are born with our way of thought, but we need our parents, to provide the nurturing, so we can learn properly.

"To start, we need love."

Don't let the pressures of life, weigh you down. Focus on the positive, and allow the setbacks to build you up for the future. Leave your past behind, that part of you is dead. You will be defined by your present, and what is seen. Your new life is formed, through the principles of God's word, and you will become a living testimony. Take every step to learn and apply it to your life.

I FOLLOWED THE LIGHT, BUT...

The Bible will teach you, that you are a conqueror, and to acknowledge, if you need help. You can't make it in your own strength, you must get into a dynamic, and energized faith-based church. Since you accepted Christ as your Lord and Savior, you are now walking in a new light. Our heavenly father equipped us with the proper fundamentals, to provide structure to your life.

You have the power to fight every obstacle, that tries to hinder your daily walk. Hold on to your spiritual connection, your life depends on it. Grasp hold of your divined dignity and never let go; you deserve greatness. The thoughts of your past should push you into your present. The present will journey you towards your future, and that's great.

"Do not continue living in the past, you will become stagnant."

I FOLLOWED THE LIGHT, BUT...

I want you to remember, to never allow anything to hold you back. The enemy will slither in, destroy your mind, and leave you clueless. He will tempt you in many ways, but I say, "stand strong and do not let that monster take you backward. Make your decision based on the principles, written in the Bible. If you don't follow it, you will regret it.

"Let's talk about making wise decisions."

Do you remember in the book of Daniel, the three Hebrew boys, Shadrach, Meshach, and Abednego? They disobeyed the request of King Nebuchadnezzar of Babylon; he told them to fall to their knees, worship his gold image, and serve his gods. Because of their disbelief, they politely disobeyed his command. The Hebrew boys, told him, the God they serve, is powerful and would deliver them from the raging flames.

King Nebuchadnezzar, grew angry, and immediately commanded his men, to throw them into the fiery furnace. When they attempted to follow his instructions, the flames killed his men, but the Hebrew boys were unharmed. When the king, looked into the furnace, he saw four men instead of three. Soon afterward, they all walked out, and the fourth man was the son of God.

They passed through the fiery furnace, and was surprised, their clothing didn't get burned. I know you're asking, why; well, it's because Jesus was in the furnace with them. I said that to say, **"don't allow people to deter your mind, into a shape of destruction. Listen to constructive words, of a godly person, their opinion has a useful purpose to build you up."** Every struggle we encounter is to strengthen and push us into our journey.

There's a war going on with our flesh and our spirit; they conflict with each other. We must read our bible, pray, not lose sight; and never give up. Whichever you yield your body to, is what will take control of your life.

Which one will you serve? Life or death, blessing or curse.

The word of God says to choose life, be encouraged and acknowledge there's a savior. Accept God as your guidance, and he will never leave nor forsake you. He will be with us every step of the way. He will teach us how to fight the good fight of faith, and to stand strong. We often wrestle, not only against our flesh and blood, but against principalities. We have to reach higher, and look beyond this dark non-spirited world, and associate with spirited people. Pay close attention to the those that could be fake.

Then we must see what their motive is; do they want to harm or tear us down? Do they want to build us up, to higher heights? A non-spirited individual is walking in darkness, and lack knowledge, of how to move towards the light. They are hurting inside, and often, want to hurt others. They want others to feel the same pain, that lives within them. Most of the time, it's mental, and emotional stress, with added turmoil.

A spirited person struggled and left the dark world, and now walk in the light with positive growth. The world of is full of evil spirits, and we are torn down, almost to the brink of death. Once we have fallen so low, we can either stay down, or rise up, and follow the light of God. The devil tried to steal my destiny and trap me from greatness.

"Always lean on God's word, for strength."

"God gives us power and authority, to overcome everything the enemy tries to devour."

The thief comes not only to steal, but to kill, and destroy.

Remember:

(1). The word of God is spirit and life.

(2). The weapons of our warfare are not carnal, but mighty through God to the pulling down of strongholds.

(3). Put on the whole armor of God, that is the only way we can stand against the wiles of the devil. We must gain control of our thinking, so our life will be made whole.

Do not let the enemy convince you, too follow him, and spoil your happiness.

I FOLLOWED THE LIGHT, BUT...

Another thing to remember is to not allow the enemy (our inner behavior) to make you weak behind human flesh. You will definitely be out of line with God's word. There are consequences that will follow your disobedience. Never think, you will win with that type of behavior because you won't. You could end up with a life-threatening disease, or much more.

Now, I know that is easier said, than done, but that's why, we must read the Bible, to get a clear understanding. It will give us strength and the will to follow the principle. Don't let your weakness, overpower, doing it the right way.

"With God, all things are possible to him that believes."

If you made the decision to follow God's word, then you must adhere, whether you want to or not.

<u>*OVERCOMERS*</u>

Chap. VI

As an adult, I now refuse to step out of the anointing, that's been placed on my life. I shall not stoop lower, and allow the enemy to take control. The spiritual warfare, that is happening today is real, it is designed to shake the minds of each individual. The evil wicked spirits enters inside and fights to turn us from spiritual to natural. This goes beyond the natural eyes, that's why we must be born again, of the spirit of God.

OVERCOMERS

The spirits can not be touched, because there is a powerful force, that blocks all unnatural behavior. Evil spirits, try to weaken our character and attack my mind.

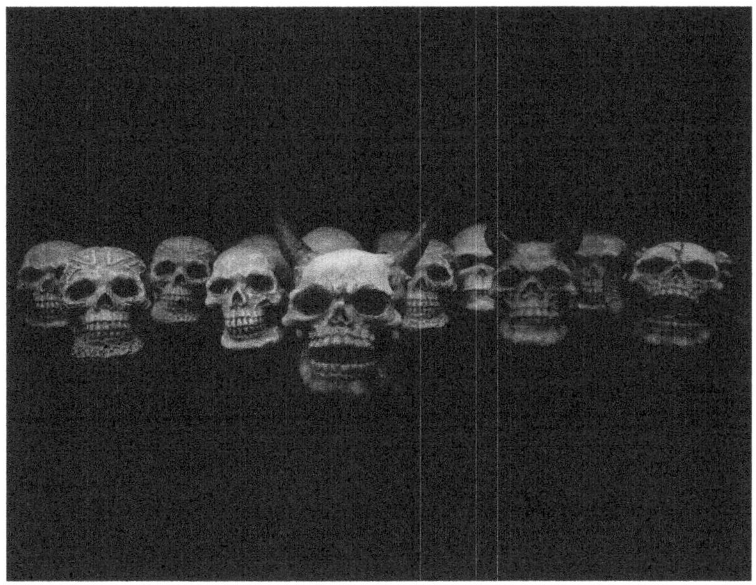

My mind wasn't stable, so I became a target. I had no direction, and became bitter, angered, and aggressive. I muttered and complained all the time, nothing was pleasing to me. My attitude caused discomfort for all, and because of that, I was miserable, and sick.

"Block the enemy with prayer."

My past tried to keep me from moving to my future. When there is an exercise of control, we will never reach our level of aim, or purpose. Also, I had another issue; procrastination, which held me back from accomplishing my goals.

"I give all the glory to God because he set me free from the grips of sin."

He allowed me to set new goals, and strive towards their reach; I moved forward. I chose to leave the old life, and focus on the whole Armour of God.

I made my decision to walk with him, in righteousness and holiness. He's always there to strengthen my faith, when someone tries to change my thoughts.

I excelled with wisdom, and saw the devil, as soon as he appeared.

John 8:12 says, "I am the light of the world, whoever follows me will not walk in darkness, but will have the light of life."

Without following the words written in the Bible, we can't see how to move in a proper direction; there is no light. To be truthful, even though I said, I was strong enough to follow my heavenly Father, my mind continued to hinder me, and made me feel differently. When I tried to complete a task, I kept saying, **"I'm not doing this, I can't make it happen."** I felt stressed because I wanted more, but taking the first step, was the hardiest; it frightened me. Well, God wouldn't accept my excuses, he kept after me until I obeyed Him.

I took the steps and thanks to Him, I can share my childhood disasters, so you can be aware of the behavior. I wrote this book to unveil the wicked spirits, that hides behind the walls of sin. We must take heed of devilish acts, that connect us, daily. Sin is detrimental, and it preys on individuals (children, adults, and seniors) that are spiritually decapitated. Also, it tries to make people impress those, that do not favor them.

People with that type of behavior, do not have a divined connection with God. Once that behavior is continued, they will dig a hole deep enough to fall in. The consequences will not be great, and suffering is brought to the forefront. Some will change and connect with the spirit of God, and others will continue playing the evil dangerous game. There is a solution whenever they are ready to move forward.

OVERCOMERS

God will create a new direction and a layout plan for us to follow. He will not beg for us to come to him, but he's ready when we're ready to be sincere. We must seek him with all our hearts, and his miraculous life-saving plan will begin. He will start on the inside, and create a dynamic image, that the world will see. When we truly seek him, he will transform a new character within us. We will walk with dignity and our head, held high.

One thing, he will not do, is condone, evil acting behavior. He does not tolerate, deliberate disobedience. Do not be fake with him, because he knows when we are not being truthful; heavy penalties will occur. He loves us, but we must understand, we will be chastised for our wrongdoings. When we accept our wrong, he will renew our mind, and then allow our journey to continue.

God's word is the key, to all our problems, his direction will teach us how to handle them. I thought I was strong, but my mind hindered, and fought me, every step of the way. I tried to maintain, but obstacles were thrown at me.

"God, what do I do?"

For example: I let some teenagers stay at my house, because I didn't want to see them on the street. I always tried to help people do better, but their stay turned out to be a disorderly disaster. Never take on extra responsibilities, until you're mentally ready. Let God work within you, so you will have the strength to lead the pack. I was not spiritually matured enough to handle, the unearthly, and dissatisfying behaviors of the young adults. ***"Get your house in order (your mind, body, and soul), before you try to work with someone else; those two don't mix!"***

We must take time, to allow our godly fruits to bear, then, our knowledge excels to greater heights. **The Fruits of the Spirit** are comprised of **love, joy, peace, long-suffering, kindness, goodness, faithfulness, gentleness, and self-control (Galatians 5:22-23).** The only way to produce is to allow God to instill the **Holy Spirit** within you. The first step happens when we believe.

Then we begin the lifelong work, by submitting to God's authority. We will grow in knowledge and learn how to walk with obedience. If we want to prosper, we must watch what we say and do. The effects of disobedience will cause a disturbance within our thought process. Also, immoral sins will stifle our ability to move forward, pornography and lustful eyes, to name a few. I realized I had to be careful, with the type of activities that occupied my intellect.

I had to learn discernment, between when God or the devil was presenting something to me.

"wickedness can be crippling"

When we have problems, our mind becomes tainted with devil antics. Our mouth opens up, like a flowing river with ungodly speech. Be careful how the image of you, is being presented to others; it could be labeled as poison. With that type of unclean spirit, we are unable to accomplish our lifelong dreams. Our mentality drops low and we do not start or finish any great ideas, we had in the beginning. The old saying is, "we get cold feet."

"Don't fear, for I have redeemed you; I have called you by name; you are Mine."

Isaiah 43:1

OVERCOMERS

When we trust and believe in the word of God, our negative thoughts will disappear. Then the positive aspects will be at the front of our mindset. Once we truly got him within our soul, it becomes anchored. At times we will fall short, with the thought of non-spiritual desires, but we must stay focused on the principles. God already knows your heart, thoughts, wants, and needs. Ask him to steer you in the right direction, and strengthen you, in the areas of weakness.

You are his prize, and he wants you to be given the best; you are so deserving of it. Our almighty Savior is merciful, and he connects us with people that have goals and ambitions. Before that can happen, we must have a personal relationship with him; otherwise, there is no connection. As an adult I learned, eternal life is an ongoing process, of development.

Another thing I know, living in the past is detrimental, it will define you. If you continue thinking, and doing the same things, your actions will never change. I'm so grateful, I was able to leave the past behind and not look back. I noticed people blame others, for their devilish behaviors; which is not one of God's principles. There are consequences, that will follow, the wrongdoings of blame, we will suffer.

Step up, and follow the spiritual guideline, and you will prosper. Allow the wisdom, God created in you, to give you the proper instructions in solving situations; think before you act. He wants to make sure the outcome, turns out for the best. We must never turn to external influences when we need circumstances resolved. First, pray to God, then, step two, the proper authorities will surface. If any additional assistance is needed, step three and so on will appear.

OVERCOMERS

"We can not solve our problems with the same level of thinking that created them."

God's plan for our life is already in place, we have to grab it, and let him carry us to destiny. That's why I tell you, about being connected to him, so you can hear what He's telling you to do. He will teach you survival skills, but you must abide by the principles of his word.

The door to your freedom is waiting, so reach out, and touch his powerful hands; he will then direct your path. He gave us two powerful doors; the first door opens our hearts up to Him. We must love and obey every inch of our mind, body, and soul. The other opens up to the world and the people around us. We must love our neighbors, the same as we love ourselves, but we must not allow them to detour our walk with God. Teach them how to help others the value of following the word.

OVERCOMERS

I've conquered many giants, as I walked through the valley, trying to get to righteousness; I am a warrior. I was determined to connect with my heavenly father; I knew he loved me.

"My command is this, Love each other as I have loved you."

John 15:12

"God wants to be involved in our everyday life; do not shut him out!"

Looking back on memories, I thought about when I lost my two precious jewels. I received a heartfelt, and devastating call about the passing of my loving mother. Then, three months later, I was stricken by the death of my husband. I received the call in January of twenty-fourteen, I went to the hospital, but made it, five minutes too late; my love was gone.

I immediately felt distraught, because my soulmate was gone. The after affect was uncomfortable, because I had to make plans to say goodbye. I had never planned for a funeral before, but I knew it had to be done. I stepped up and started the process. I took the word of God as my lead and everything fell in proper order. I proceeded with diligence, and, my love was laid to rest in the utmost way.

Why, because when you have a connection with the highest God, he will lead and guide you. Where I should have been broken and shattered, I was calm.

"You will keep in perfect peace those whose minds are steadfast because they trust in you."

Isaiah 26:3

Blessings from God is special and worthy of the divined treatment. We must appreciate the gifts he sacrificed for us, he loves us. He sits high and looks low, watching everything that concerns our well-being. The principles of God's word, assures us not to worry.

1st Peter 5:7 says, "Cast all your anxiety on Him, because he cares for you."

When we are troubled in our spirit, we have to pick ourselves up real fast. Do not sit around being sad, or feeling the need to go backwards; stand strong. God will comfort us in the time of need. Remember, dark days will always come, but instead of it sending you to a pit, allow it to make you rise above, and into the light. Take your negative experiences, and turn them into a positive; then look back and see your growth.

OVERCOMERS

When you see your achievements, you will be astounded by your God given success.

Psalms 46:1 reads, "God is our refuge and strength, a very present help in trouble."

When we beat our struggles, we will succeed in defeating the difficult obstacles. Substance abuse, alcoholism, psychological setbacks, and much more, are major life wreckers. Families are being torn apart by the devastating downfalls of using substances, to pacifier their hurt and pain.

What I mean is, if we have to use something to ease our unpleasant sensations, we will never grow in God's word. We must remember to stand when we're being tackled by a hard play, or the hurdle we thought we couldn't jump over. Once we take the leap of faith and master it, we're ready to move to a new level. All we have to do, is talk to our heavenly father, he will give us direction.

He will also lift us, when we've been torn down; but we must believe. From experience, I can tell you, we can not overcome our problems by ourselves, we need the power of our creator.

"Attack your problems head-on."

I remember when I was eight years old, I received my first bible. I couldn't understand the words, but if I knew then, what I know now, my life would have gone in a different direction. I now realize every word written, was for a reason. It would have saved me a lot of heartache and pain. Instead of reading it, I slept with it under my pillow, thinking it would keep the devil away.

Now that I'm older, I know the bible is full of living power, it's sharp as a dagger. It also, cuts deep and into our soul. We will learn, who loves us, without conditions, **God is Love.**

OVERCOMERS

Our lives are considered an open book, we were born with purity and then as we experienced life, it became unraveled. Once it is torn apart, the manifestation of unclean impurities is shown. What I mean by that, the enemy tries to include us, in his many dirty tactics, especially when we are not spiritually empowered. When we're put in a position, to choose the proper decision, we struggle tremendously.

We want to do right, but evil presents itself, and we get caught up in the middle; then an unjust character is presented. God shines upon those that have no problem being strong, and standing for what is right. If we want to prosper, we must be embedded with his word.

John 4:4 states, "You, dear children, are from God and have overcome them, because the one who is in you is greater than the one who is in the world."

OVERCOMERS

I remember the times when I was depressed, broken and shattered; my soul was weak. I was so down I wanted to be alone all the time. I felt like no one cared, so I turned away from the people, that truly loved me. I also saw people that I thought were my friends, but they appeared to be talking about me. When I came near them, they stopped talking.

I felt uncomfortable because if they were my friends, they should have noticed, I was having some situations. I had to realize, everyone wasn't like me, I knew when something was wrong. God wants us to pay attention, and be aware, of the needs of others. I almost allowed those negative thoughts, to enter my mind, and distract my feelings towards them.

"In tough situations, we must ask God to show us what to do, and how to make a gracious attempt to complete it."

We must also help others, that have not adapted to the right process; showing interest, becomes a bond. God's principles speak about the ***Fruits of the Spirit***, we are the fruit and what we possess inside, is the spirit. The Bible spoke about nine fruits, that we're supposed to apply to our daily lives.

God also reminds us that the most powerful fruit is love. He brought life into existence, with divined freshness; we are blessed. He loved us so much, that he gave up his only son, Jesus Christ, to die, so we could live. In knowing how unselfish he was, is indeed the greatest blessing. That's why we must love him and all that he created.

"Above all, love each other deeply, because love covers over a multitude of sins."

1 Peter 4:8

Often, we are faced with trials, tribulations, and troubles; past and present. When those times occur, we must ask God to strengthen us. Our struggles become bearable because we think of ways to cope. It seems easier said than done, because when situations arise, our adrenaline began to flow, and we forget about what we've learned.

I remember having major surgery, and due to the severity of my medical problem, I was diagnosed with Clinical Depression. Before then, I didn't understand what was going on. I thought I was losing my mind, I became fearful, thinking I couldn't worship God anymore. The thought of my diagnosis haunted me, I couldn't sleep at night. Fear followed me in the daytime, and I couldn't stop crying. All of a sudden I heard, **"stop the crying, get your praise on, and worship me."**

I heard the sound and knew that was God talking to me. I continued the feeling until I finally settled down, I felt much better. I started doing my Jericho marching dance, I ended up outside, jogging and praying. I was excited because, God told me, to dry up my tears and lean on him. I ran up and down the street, with a strong strut and loud praise. I was energized and ready!

I looked up and saw my neighbor watching, and I wondered what she was thinking. Days later, I felt so good I decided to visit her. I told her who I was and she said, "I see you walking and talking, all through the day." I said, "yes, that's my communication time with the Lord." I started talking to her about the goodness of Jesus, and I started crying. I felt bad because I had no clue, she had health issues. I was just being friendly, like God instructed me to do.

I didn't act as fast as I should have, but I knew she wasn't a person of God. When I saw her hurting, it touched me.

"A single act of kindness throws out roots in all directions, and the roots spring up and make new trees."

As an over-comer, we must show them, how to lean on the power of our father. He is the only one that can help us.

Proverbs 18:24 says, "One who has unreliable friends, soon comes to ruin, but there is a friend who sticks closer than a brother."

That day we became friends, and I started visiting her more. I prayed and read the bible, and she began to enjoy it. Our praise and worship time lasted for years, then she passed away. I was so happy, I was able to ease her pain, and to be truthful, she eased mine as well. We helped each other, I enjoyed talking to her.

One day I ran into Lara, an old co-worker, and she told me how much Brenda enjoyed me spending time with her. Lara also said, she told her, I was her best friend, and she loved the way, I spoke about God. I was surprised because I never knew I touched her soul. I didn't get the chance to let her know, how much she touched me, as well.

Then another day, I walked into the post office, and was greeted so kindly. The postmaster said, “you're Judy, Brenda's friend, right?” I responded, “yes, she was my neighbor.” He then said, “she used to talk about you all the time.” I was shocked; tears came streaming down my face, because I didn't think she cared, about me that much.

Let me tell you, when we do what's in our heart, that's pure love. God blesses us, when we step out of ourselves, and show concern for someone else. He connected us for a remarkable reason; we helped each other. I was grateful, she taught me a lesson.

Colossians 3:23-24 states, “Whatever you do, work at it with all your heart, as working for the Lord, not for human masters. Since you know that you will receive an inheritance from the Lord as a reward, It is the Lord Christ you are serving.

We never know who's suffering from something. We should never allow, the way they look, to deter us from presenting, the ***Fruits of the Spirit.*** In the midst of helping my friend Brenda, my episodes of depression lessened. My heavenly Father showed me, how to take the focus off of my situations, and give attention to her. He also told me, that would help cure me. My battle continued after I received some tragic news.

My only son was shot half to death, piercing a hole in his side. When I saw him in the hospital, everything inside of me, got more intense. I knew I had obstacles, that I had to deal with, I looked beyond myself, and focused on my son. I was determined to not allow stress and depression, to keep me down. I began praying and praising to God, I asked him to restore my son's life. I believed, my prayers would be answered, all I needed was faith.

The enemy tried to break me down, lower than before. I heard many negative comments, from the doctors. They said, there was a possibility, he wouldn't survive. The bullet was lodged close to his spine, and there was a possibility, of him being paralyzed, for the rest of his life. For that reason, they didn't try removing the bullet. I trusted in the word of God, that my son would live.

He received special care, and weeks later, he walked out of the hospital. He continued therapy, and within three months, he was cleared, to return to work. I gave all my attention to him and my depression subsided. He carried out his daily task, with the bullet next to his spine. He asked for prayer, for it to be removed, without causing internal damage. God answered his prayer on Father's day, the bullet fell from his back to his foot.

My heavenly Father completed the surgery; I knew he would. He returned to the doctor, and they were surprised; the test proved, there was no bullet. They said that had never happened before, I said, "it was God."

"For I will restore Health to you and heal you of your wounds."

Jeremiah 30:17

Often, before we accept our Lord and Savior, we create a traumatizing experience, that leaves us with doubt. We think we can do things the way we want, and live a double life. The problem with that, it's negative and will cause confusion.

OVERCOMERS

When we're living without spiritual guidance, we're faced with unbearable situations. I lived in darkness, and saw the unearthly path of the devil and traveled that road. I should have stayed on my spiritual path, and followed the road of righteousness. I did everything the devil told me to do, and I almost lost my life. My disobedience involved me in three different scary incidents; all involved a gun.

The first time, I received a knock at my door. When I answered it, I saw a man, standing there holding a gun. He then lifted it, and pointed it at me; I was terrified. The man stood there for a minute, staring at me; he appeared to be spaced out. He then walked away with his head held down. I down know what that was all about, but God saved my life that night. The next day, I was informed, that the gunman said, the way I was dressed, I was on my way to church.

I thought that was weird, but I thanked my heavenly Father, for protecting me. Sometimes, we can look at people and see their light of Christianity. That could have been what the gunman saw, in me; all I could do was give praises to God. The second time, I went to someone's house, and the conversation we had, didn't go so well. We started arguing, and a gun was pulled out on me. I didn't fear for my life, so I kept talking.

Finally, we stopped, and he put the gun back in his pocket. As soon as I got home, I received a call, the enemy shot himself in the leg. I don't know if he meant to shoot himself, or if it was an accident. The third incident happened, when I told a guest at my house, they had to leave. I was tired of living in darkness, and I needed my life back. The individual refused to listen to me, and we started fighting.

I wasn't fearful of him, even though I knew he had a gun. I stood firm, and he finally realized I was serious. He said, "Oh, so you're for real, holy roller?" I said, "yes I am, you need to leave."

God said, "Call upon Me in the day of trouble; I will deliver you, and you shall glorify Me."

Psalms 50:15

He slammed the door in my face, and later I was informed, he went back to his house, and shot it up. He almost killed the occupant that lived there. I was so grateful that he didn't kill me, he had the gun pointed at my face. I was tired of the dark life and chose to finally serve God. I gave my mind, body, and soul to him. After many days and nights, of heavy thoughts, my heavenly Father took me into the marvelous light. I am so thankful, he protected me from harm.

My gratefulness still stands today, I saw how unhappy God was when I was a start and stop Christian. I lived a double life, and that was a displeasure to both of us. He didn't give up on me, and I learned through my consequences, I could not live like that. Straddling the fence. was tiresome and stressful; I caused all my pain. If it wasn't for the grace and mercy of God, I wouldn't be here today.

If you want to be set free, from the clutches of hell, you must cry out to God, for his help; you can't do it by yourself. I know this is the truth because I kept falling backward until I changed. I finally accepted the light and followed it with sincerity. I thought I could handle, life on my own, but that was far from the truth. I found out, no matter what I done or who I went to, I wasn't released until I surrendered to Jesus. Nothing else worked, and that's the truth.

OVERCOMERS

As we get older, we learn how traumatic, disobedient behavior can be. Let's talk about obedience, it is a positive behavior, that's respectful and mindful of rules and laws. When we do what we're told, we are following God's authority. We are his servants and must pay attention to his principles, We must also abide by them, and our life will flourish. The great book says, we must listen to what others have to say.

Often, we take the easy route, we talk and help those close to us, but do not reach out to people that we don't personally know. We were created to be leaders, and not followers, unless it is a positive move. We are supposed to step out, of our normal life, and help those, that are suffering from abnormalities. God welcomes the unjust, and we're supposed to do the same. I told him I would help everybody, so I opened up my home, gave food, and clothes.

I also helped fulfill financial necessities, to the homeless. You would think, they would be grateful; some yes, some no. I remember one particular time, I fell on hard times, some of the people that I helped, walked all over me, like I was nothing. Right then, I learned, some people will take advantage, of those with a kind heart. Their spiritual attributes are looked upon as a gateway to weakness. I'm glad I was grounded by the word, because I could have suffered from deep emotional hurt.

I thanked God, for allowing me, to be his soldier of Christ. I knew I was engaged in spiritual warfare and needed to fight the enemy, the right way. My strength in the Lord showed me how to deal with people that possess ungodly non-caring character. I educated them with the word and shared my testimonies. After a while, not only did I help them, but I rose above the ill feelings.

OVERCOMERS

We must not allow anything, or anyone to make us fall beneath our worth. When we rise to the top, we will often see the same people, that passed us by. They might need assistance; God principles, commanded us, to help them, again. We are not to look at what they did in the past, we are to cherish them, for what they are now. Our blessings flow when we're not holding grudges, back-biting, or seeking revenge.

Everyone is not going to care for us, but we must remain the person God created us to be. Our character will always reveal who we are, and if we're not possessing spiritual attributes. Put your trust in the master, and he will direct your path. He will change your thoughts and give you a new impression. Once you have accepted and stood bold, the master, will grant you peace, joy, and understanding. Also, you will adapt to your new life and the changes that come with it.

OVERCOMERS

Some people, we call friends, will walk away when they see a different person within us. Do not fret the small stuff, God will handle that. When He picks the new people, for us to associate with, they will be on a higher level. He will make sure, we are equipped with the best. He will also, generate enhanced knowledge, wisdom, understanding, and financial stewardship. Some people, he will not allow, to stay in our circle, because they are not compatible with our spirituality.

When I was a child, I was told my life wouldn't amount to anything. I told myself, I would make that statement false, and I would rise above the attacks of the enemy. God did not allow me to fall down and never get up. I learned from the negative experiences and excelled to the utmost. The struggle is real, but we must never give up, trouble doesn't last always.

OVERCOMERS

I am so grateful for all my past experiences. The old saying is, "The harder they press, the greater the test, and only the strong survive." When you run into people, that present unethical behavior, show them there is a better way to live. Sometimes, we need to be reminded, where we came from. We must never look down, at the ones, that are not on our level; help them up. Show them how to rise above the negativity.

You're with Jesus now, and nothing no one says or do will make you lose your focus. Don't pay attention to them, stand strong, and listen to the word of God. Many times, I wished, I had somebody I could go to, for direction. I struggled with troubles, of making the wrong decisions. I turned to a tarot card reader, to give me a clear understanding, of what was happening. At that time, I didn't know it was wrong, so my situation ended up in a disaster.

I turned to the world of darkness, like wizards, and got involved in a cult. They worshiped in unusual religion, spiritual, and philosophical beliefs. I put my trust in people with toxic methods. We are not supposed to connect with abnormal, and deadly doings; Jesus is our everything. He is the way, the truth, and the life. Satan will appear as an angel of light, to deceive us with false religion.

Many are unaware of what is being spoken, that's why their lives are destroyed. Only in the words of God, we will find the true light. The one and only guide will give us direction, through the toughest times. If you believe in Jesus, and accept him in your life, he will direct your path. You must abide by his word, and not falter when you encounter discomforts. Trust me I had to learn from my unsteady behavior. I turned away from the principles when I had major setbacks.

"Turning away from your problems, is not the proper thing to do, nothing else will save you, but the word."

We need God's spiritual nourishment, so we can live a prosperous life, and become successful. Some people disagree and do not think he is worth their time. When ***disasters happen, then they can not cope.*** They want to settle matters with violence and unjustly actions; that is unethical behavior. The principles of God's word is the opposite, we learn how to handle it, with dignity and poise.

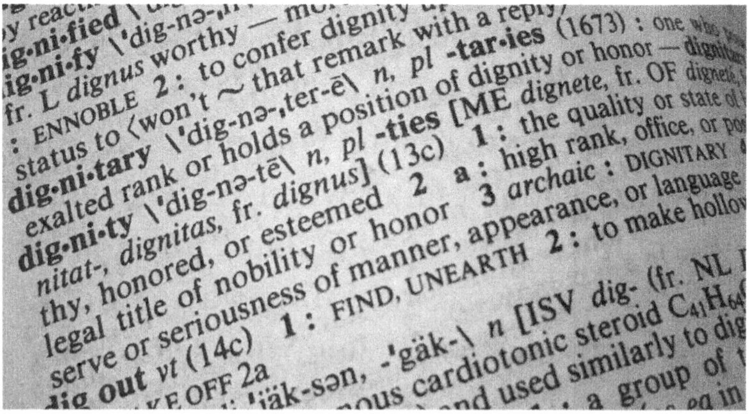

prosperity
respect
dignity
equality
reliability
freedom
responsibility
peace
justice
hope
faith

HOPE
DESPAIR

OVERCOMERS

We must remember, God is powerful and he created us in his image. He gave us life, which is remarkable, and we should cherish it with every breath we blow. Life is a long slow race, we must continue until we've mastered to the end. It takes a long time to accomplish and win the race. Those that stand strong, swift, and determined, will win. Those that procrastinate, are lazy, and make excuses, will stop in the middle, (strength comes from our mind).

In order to not give up, when the race gets hard, we must be connected to a power source. For example, the electricity we need, supplies light, it must have a connection. Once the is plugged in, energy is restored, but if the connection has no power, it will not provide energy. When we're connected to the right source, our spirit is humbled. We must be attentive, seek, and have the desire to achieve.

God is our Powerful connection.

Once we have our minds, in the right place, then we're ready to run the race. If we link up with the wrong source, no connection is available; no power.

I think about the bittersweet time (salty in the beginning, and sweet in the end) when I finally reunited with my mother. I went to live with her and enjoyed the wonderful life we shared together. Sometimes, there were emotional feelings, but I got through them. After a while, I became independent and moved into my own place. Months later, she lost her home to an electrical fire. The fire started in the area where my children and I, slept.

I was so grateful, that the Lord spared our lives, he protected us from hurt and harm. He took care of us, and not allowed us, to be sleep, when the tragedy happened. I praised my precious Lord because my children would always visit my mother, but this time they were with me. When I received the news, I knew it was God's protection that saved us. We lost items but were replaced by our heavenly angels.

One day, I received a visit from my little girl's teacher. She gave me her sympathy, for our loss, and then gave me new clothes for her. She said she wanted to do something nice; because she loved her. Once the word got around, I received groceries from unknown sources, with the label, "Love Offering." Tears rolled down my cheeks because my cupboards were almost bare.

I always said, "it may not come when I want it, but it's always on time." God supplied all my needs according to His riches in glory. His angels watched over us and took charge.

Jehovah Jireh - "The Lord will see to it - He will provide."

Genesis 22:14

Lift my hands unto the Lord, from where all my help comes from.

...God is my Provider...

...God is my Healer...

...God is my Everything...

To tell you how grateful I was, when my daughter was two years old, she experienced difficulties with her sight. I knew I wasn't practicing, Christian principles, but I was concerned.

OVERCOMERS

I walked into a church and asked for prayer. I explained to the preacher, that I was not grounded, but needed help for my small child. He didn't hesitate to pray and then gave me suggestions, about getting on track with God, our Savior. He said, "God is a healer, and is always present, to keep us calm when heavy storms occur." I wasn't locked down in my mind and heart, as to what he said, but the thought remained.

He told me, I must join a faith-based church, so my soul would strengthen and grow. I thanked him and went on my way. I was so happy, because, as times went on, she got healed. I can truly tell you when we seek God, we will find him. He's always ready with His arms wide open. I thought about what the preacher told me, and I finally realized, he was right. Other's told me the same thing, plus I already knew what to do, because I leaned on God before.

I knew he was a healer, and that he was always present, to keep us calm when obstacles hindered us. I also knew how to lift my hands to him, cause that was where all my help came from. I told myself to stop back-sliding, and move forward. I later stood firm and said, **"God is my provider, God is my healer, God is my everything."**

My brothers and sisters, listen to me, when trouble meets you head-on, don't try and fight the beast; you will never win. Turn to the master, that has the power, to fight your battles. Get out of his way, cause he got everything, and we have nothing. You don't have to have the last word in a heated conversation, walk away, and hold your peace. When the dark world, gives you and your family hard challenges, pray harder, and maintain the love for them. You will finally see the light, appear, so follow it and blessings will occur.

OVERCOMERS

I remember, when I was trapped in the shadows of darkness, I was drained and overwhelmed. I had a thought of never being free; I was sad. No matter what happened to me, I still didn't give up. I kept praying and pressing forward. The feeling of being trapped put me in an undesirable condition. When I finally unleashed from the strong violent force of the devil, I realized the battle was within me.

I was held captive in my mind, where my thoughts and perceptions are perceived. When I finally broke free, of the disgusting strongholds, I told my God, I would not allow anyone to puncture my beliefs, ever again. The horrible life I experienced, taught me what not to do in the future. I went through many ups and downs before I settled. Remember, we can not do ungodly mischief and expect divined results. That is a true statement, I experienced it.

OVERCOMERS

I couldn't see or touch the unclean spirits, but they had me chained and almost destroyed. I thank our heavenly Father, for delivering me from the darkness of sin. Before deliverance, I had a lack of knowledge, obedience, and understanding. When God stepped in, he changed my negative, into a positive.

We were not created, to just let life, amount to nothing. We have an abundance of mental attributes, to offer our future leaders. We were blessed with the ability to think logical, and excel in the essentials for success.

God made us with the ability to instruct and to be instructed. Our experiences, are used as a testimony, to help lift others, from the pit of hell. They will rise into the marvelous light, and journey towards success. When we desire to help educate less fortunate individuals, our father is pleased. But, when we overlook them, we become selfish and soon will relapse back into sin. My advice is to stand firm and apply pressure to the open wound of the dark challenges.

"Do not let it weigh you down"

Unclean spirits, is a death, waiting to happen, do not allow them to affect your mind, body, and soul. Think about the book of Samuel, and how David and Goliath, had many challenges. I'm going to explain why we are plagued with so many heavy difficulties. David is often referred to, as a character in the Bible, who was known to be a man after God's heart.

In reality, history tells us that David was an actual flesh-and-blood man, with all of the failings and shortcomings, of other men. You've probably heard the story, where David killed a fearsome man, a huge soldier in the Philistine army (whom many called a "giant"). He took his slingshot, with one stone and knocked him to the ground. David's life was filled with soaring highs, such as that account, and with miserable lows, even as the king of Israel.

He wasn't perfect, so what made him different from other men, of the time? No matter what his circumstance was, David loved God and walked closely with Him. He always talked to Him in prayer and song (the entire book of Psalms in the Old Testament consists of letters and songs, David wrote to God). He praised him even during his highest highs and lowest lows. He worshiped his master since he was a boy.

OVERCOMERS

When David took his last breath, he still served God with everything he owned. In all things, David trusted our Savior, and that's what we must do. On the other hand, Goliath was the opposite, he mocked the Israelite's, and challenged them, to match one of their soldiers, against him. He stood head and shoulders above other men, garbed in heavy bronze, his shield-bearer always in front of him.

The Israelite's were afraid of Goliath, and his challenge. Even David's older brothers, who were engaged in the battle, were discouraged. Who among them could slay this giant? In this war, David was a simple Shepard, too young to join the battle lines. His father asked him, one day to carry bread and cheese, to his brothers on the front lines. In doing so, David heard Goliath, bellowing and mocking his challenge, and asked who the giant was.

David wanted to know, what would be done for the man who answered the bold challenge. When his brother's heard of David's presence and questions, they called him wicked and shamed him for not tending to he sheep, as he was told. Undaunted, David answered his brothers, and the other soldiers, by saying, he faced bears and lions, with his bare hands. He didn't have any fear, because God was his protection.

Surely he could face the giant and enjoy God's protection in defense of Israel. The most overlooked, yet most important part of this historical account is: ***David accepted Goliath's challenge.*** King Saul, offered David heavy armor and a sword, to prepare to face the dreaded giant. Uncomfortable in the heavy garb, David opted for just his Shepard's clothing. He chose five smooth stones from the riverbank, and his sling. He was ready to face the giant.

When Goliath saw him, a young boy, coming to face him, with only the sling and stones. He laughingly vowed not to only kill him, but to feed his flesh and bones, to the wild animals. David stood his ground, and looked squarely at Goliath, vowing to slay him, not with his own strength and skills, but with the power of the Lord God. With those words, David hurled a stone at Goliath and struck a single death blow, to the giant's head.

Trusting in God's strength and protection, David fearlessly faced the giant, that had terrorized an entire army for forty days. He did not brag, he put on the armor of God, and trusted Him, to carry him through the battle, just as he did before. Whether tending to his flock or facing a terrifying giant, David turned to God, for strength and courage. **Always wear the whole armor of God.**

OVERCOMERS

I said that to say, heavy obstacles, will continue, trying to block our success, but we must stand bold. We must know God will fight our battle. For example, the biggest giant we are faced with, is the lack of financial stability. The economy is steadily rising, and the income is little to none. When people experience downfalls, their ability to understand becomes detrimental. They can not see anything, but failure.

I am grateful, because I didn't allow the giants, to get the best of me. I vowed to slay each and every one of them, that tries to attack my integrity. People, we must get a grip on reality, and realize, life is what we make of it. It will not come easy, and if it does, it will not be appreciated. We won't learn from it and will backslide. We have to take every step for ourselves, and stop looking for everyone to pick up our pieces. Go to God, not people.

OVERCOMERS

There is high praise when we communicate with our heavenly Father, to pick up our pieces.

"The mind and body communicate constantly. What the mind thinks, perceives, and experiences, is sent from our brain to the rest of the body."

Hebert Benson, M.D. The Benson – Henson Institute for Mind-Body Medicine.

Parents, getting back to education, for our children, we must inform them about everything life has to offer. Our job is to start at home, with spiritual nourishment. Once they get older and depart from you, they will know how to survive, the sins of this wicked world. We must teach them how to be positive and confident.

OVERCOMERS

When accomplishing their tasks, goals, and, dreams, we must walk with them every step of the way. Let them journey into the world, knowing what and what not to do.

I was abused and went through many obstacles, that tried to kill me. I encountered many setbacks, because of my disobedient behavior. Through the teachings, I received an awakening, I saw my life being slim to none. Thanks to God I overcame my darkness and established life again.

When we are not walking with the principles of God's word, our lives are wracked with confusion. Our soul is torn, and we turn to drugs, alcohol, or even multiple unprotected sex partners. Because of our pain, our self-esteem falls low, and we give up. We suffer from depression and bitterness and after a while, it becomes to the forefront of our lives. My question is, **"How many people do you think, fall and get back up?"** I have another question, **"Why it so hard to stay focused on the word of God."**

Let me tell you why, at age nineteen, I met a male friend, through another person, whom I thought was my best friend. The guy had brown cat eyes and was very appealing. We talked for several months, and then I learned he had dropped out of school and had many hidden agendas. Even though I felt leery, we continued our connection. To make a long story short, I was wrong.

The guy I thought was so nice, turned out to be ruthless. I saw the red flags, but ignored them. I suffered the consequences, of the unwise choice I made, my flesh took control. **I can say, "when we make our bed hard, we have to deal with the uncomfortable feeling."** If I had thought of the positive aspect of being in a relationship, my actions would have been different.

I should have not focused on the outer covering, but kept my mind on the principles of God's word. I learned, that before I can bring anyone else into my circle, my life has to be complete. Once we're at full potential, we expect greater, we stand firm, on our expectations. We must tell them upfront, about our morals, standards, and righteous values. If they are worthy of a conversation, they will come correct. If he/she is not spiritually empowered, do not be quick to get involved.

Let them know you're a person, that worships the principles. If he/she, truly wants to be with you, they will adhere to the word. Never let looks, blind your mind. Our heavenly Father was with me, during the times, I was acting foolish; my decisions were unjust. I praised him because he kept trying to get my attention; and I must say, he succeeded. Sometimes I reminisce, about my past life, I use my testimonies, to witness, and help someone, that is currently struggling.

Beware, because after I graduated from high school, I became the target of a predator. I didn't see any signs, but the feeling I got made me leery of him. He offered me a job out of town, but I declined. Well, I'm glad I made the proper decision, because, I found out, the man was picked up, for sex trafficking. He was the owner of a strip club, and his motive was not right.

All I can say is, ***"God is good,"*** that could have been a detrimental situation. We go through many storms until we mature. Then we know, we must follow the word's of our Father; nothing else will work. When we have parents, with a spiritual connection, we learn how to cope with reality. We also learn, for protection, we must put on the whole Armour of God. I know you're wondering, why should we do that. The answer is, so we can stand against the wiles of the devil.

Since there is an ongoing spiritual warfare, we must keep our Bible open, and ready to resist the evil spirits. We are equipped with tools to defeat the enemy, that try to demolish our soul. ***"No weapon formed against you shall prosper, and every tongue which rises against you in judgment, shall be condemned. This is the heritage of the servants of the Lord, and their righteousness is from Me."* Isaiah 54:17**

Those that are ill-equipped with no tools, or has faulty tools, will do great harm to themselves and others. We must stand strong, and the enemy will flee.

"*A Message from God*"

1 John 4:7-9 "Dear Friends, let us love one another, for love comes from God. Everyone who loves, has been born of God, and knows Him. Whoever does not love, does not know Him, because He is love."

"This is how God showed his love among us: He sent his one and only Son, into the world that we might live through him."

Why did Jesus Die?

Jesus died so that humans could have their sins forgiven, and receive endless life (Romans 6:23; Ephesians 1:7). Jesus' death, also proved, that a human can remain loyal to God, even when faced with the severest of tests (Hebrews 4:15). The first human, Adam, was created perfect, without sin. However, he chose to disobey God. His disobedience affected, all his descendants.

Through the disobedience of one man, the Bible explains, “many were made sinners, of the one man, so also through the obedience of the one man, the many will be made righteous (Romans 5:19). He is the atoning sacrifice for our sins, and not only for ours, but also the sins of the whole world.. (1 John 2:2) Adam's disobedience contaminated the human family with sin, so Jesus' death removed the stain, from all who exercise faith in him.

In a sense, Adam sold the human race into sin. Jesus by willingly dying on our behalf repurchased humankind as his own. As a result, if anyone sin, we have a helper with the Father, Jesus Christ, a righteous one. (1 John 2:1) Although Adam was created to live forever, his sin brought upon him the penalty of death. Through Adam, sin entered into the world and death through sin, and so death spread to all men because they had all sinned. **“We are sinners saved by grace, through faith, and not by ourselves.”**

(Romans 5:12) Jesus's death not only removed the blemish of sin, but canceled the death sentence.

The End!

"I am so grateful for the opportunity, to share my childhood struggles. I hope my masterpiece, helps educate you and your children, about the importance of walking in the shadows of God's word."

"We might not want to follow instructions and directions, but we later find out, if we were obedient in the beginning, time would have been saved. May God continue blessing you and stay tuned for book # II."

"There's More to Life than what you See."

~Judy C. Linzy
Creative Image Author

Made in the USA
Columbia, SC
06 February 2020

87549891R00117